# KRISTINA TROTT

# THE
# POWER
## YOU HAVE AVAILABLE

In the battle for your mind, body and soul

thewingsofadove.com

Published in Australia by Trott Publishing,
PO Box 216, Mona Vale 2103

First published in Australia 2021
This edition published 2021

Copyright © Kristina Trott 2021

Cover design: David Brewer
Author photo: Daisy Stockbridge Photography
Typesetting: WorkingType (www.workingtype.com.au)

All Scripture quotations, unless otherwise indicated, are taken from the New King James Version®. Copyright © 1982 by Thomas Nelson. Used by permission. All rights reserved.

Scripture quotations marked (NIV) are taken from the Holy Bible, New International Version®, NIV®. Copyright © 1973, 1978, 1984, 2011 by Biblica, Inc.® Used by permission of Zondervan. All rights reserved worldwide. www.zondervan.com The "NIV" and "New International Version" are trademarks registered in the United States Patent and Trademark Office by Biblica, Inc.®

Scripture quotations marked (AMP) are taken from the Amplified Bible, Copyright © 1954, 1958, 1962, 1964, 1965, 1987 by The Lockman Foundation. Used by permission.

Scripture quotations marked (NLT) are taken from the Holy Bible, New Living Translation, copyright © 1996, 2004, 2007, 2013, 2015 by Tyndale House Foundation. Used by permission of Tyndale House Publishers, Inc., Carol Stream, Illinois 60188. All rights reserved.

Scripture quotations marked Message are taken from THE MESSAGE, copyright © 1993, 2002, 2018 by Eugene H. Peterson. Used by permission of NavPress. All rights reserved. Represented by Tyndale House Publishers, a Division of Tyndale House Ministries.

Scripture quotations marked (Jer.Bib) are taken from the JERUSALEM BIBLE Copyright© 1966, 1967, 1968 by Darton, Longmand & Todd LTD and Doubleday and Co. Inc. All rights reserved.

Scripture quotations marked (KJV) are taken from the KING JAMES VERSION, public domain.

The right of Kristina Trott to be identified as the Author of the Work has been asserted in accordance with the Copyright, Designs and Patents Act 1988.

All rights reserved. No part of this publication may be reproduced, stored in a retrieval system, or transmitted, in any form or by any means without the prior written permission of the publisher, nor be otherwise circulated in any form of binding or cover other than that in which it is published and without a similar condition being imposed on the subsequent purchaser.

This Manuscript is the property of the author. It should not under any intentions be copied or reproduced without copyright allowance. Nor should the person engaged with the document change the content for their personal gain.

Kristina Trott
*The Power You Have Available*
ISBN:9780646830162
pp254

*In memory of my precious friend,*
*Yang Soon (Sue) Golafshan 1952-2014*

# Contents

| | | |
|---|---|---|
| Introduction | | v |
| Chapter 1 | God Saves Me From a Cult | 1 |
| Chapter 2 | In Love God Seeks to Save You | 20 |
| Chapter 3 | The Power of the Holy Spirit | 31 |
| Chapter 4 | The Devil Makes Himself Known | 43 |
| Chapter 5 | Communion with God | 49 |
| Chapter 6 | Evicted From the Cult | 67 |
| Chapter 7 | Discovering that Jesus Heals Today | 75 |
| Chapter 8 | The Diagnosis of Cancer | 83 |
| Chapter 9 | The Power of Your Faith | 90 |
| Chapter 10 | The Power of Prayer for Healing | 124 |
| Chapter 11 | The Power of Words of Hope | 131 |
| Chapter 12 | The Power Over the Devil | 140 |
| Chapter 13 | The Power of the Name | 158 |
| Chapter 14 | The Power of Your Praise | 164 |
| Chapter 15 | The Power of Communion | 172 |
| Chapter 16 | The Cancer Has Gone! | 182 |
| Chapter 17 | The Power of His Resurrection | 185 |
| Chapter 18 | Who Gets Custody of Your Emotional Health? | 189 |
| Chapter 19 | The Worst — Losing Hair and Losing LOTS of Hair | 208 |
| Chapter 20 | The Power of Prayer for a Husband | 211 |
| Chapter 21 | The PET Scan Confirms the Cancer Has Gone | 217 |
| Chapter 22 | The Power of Your Amen | 223 |
| Chapter 23 | It's a Wild Journey | 235 |

## Introduction

*"For the kingdom of God
is not in word but in power."*
(I Cor. 4:20)

In the middle of Sydney Harbour, about a kilometre from the Sydney Opera House, is a sandstone outcrop known locally as Pinchgut. It is said that it was given this name when reoffending convicts in the late eighteenth century were sent to this rocky island, shackled in irons and fed a starvation diet of bread and water. Escape from the prison was nigh on impossible.

This prison, however, isn't as bad as the prison many people in this world are in. Pinchgut could only confine the body, but there are shackles that confine the mind of a person and place them in dungeons far more frightening than anything a person could create.

I was in a self-imposed prison.

I was born into a cult that rejected Christian doctrines and had a very different Jesus.

My life was prescribed by the rules of the cult and any

association with people or activities outside the cult was frowned upon.

I became a Christian, but not all of the bondages from the cult disappeared.

After 43 years and 6 children and gut-wrenching circumstances, my husband announced that our marriage was over.

I felt discarded and worthless.

I wanted to die.

And then I developed incurable cancer and faced a few short months before I was told I would die.

Except that wasn't the end of my story. I had to learn and believe that God saw me as valuable. I had to learn to be free. I had to learn to forgive. And I didn't die. In fact, all signs of the cancer miraculously disappeared a few weeks after diagnosis and, to top it all off, I found my soul mate who treats me with all the love and respect I had never had.

And the secret? It was giving myself entirely over to Jesus, knowing who He was, what He had done for every person on this planet and being fully confident that He was still the same today, that I was healed from all of my sins, shame, guilt, emotional pain and disease.

I didn't deserve this love from Jesus. I was loved purely and simply because of the incredible grace of God that He has poured out on us. It wasn't anything I had done that caused God to call me His daughter. God wants us no matter what we have done or how we have failed. He delights in setting us free from our past and restoring all that we have lost. He is a good, good Father — far better than the best of any earthly fathers. But if you didn't have an earthly father or even if you had a ghastly earthly father, He has promised to be an all-surpassing Father to the fatherless.

As a son or daughter of the living God, this is your real identity. It is irrelevant what people say about you or even what you say about yourself. God sees you as His child and that is that! There is no higher position that you could ever aspire to.

Once you realise what is in God's heart, you will never be the same again. You can't ever go back to feeling afraid or disheartened. You can't be angry and bitter. Once you comprehend that you've been lavished with abundant love from none other than the God of the universe, you will want to share that love with everyone you meet.

I want you to know that God wants to be your Father — He

wants to love you and offer you the power to free you from your fears, pain and sickness today. Finding out about that power and working with that power is what this book is all about. I am writing this book just for you. Do you want to be set free from a past that haunts you? Are you navigating a life that is beset with problems? Are you suffering with an unrelenting sickness? Are you overwhelmed and pessimistic about an inescapably dismal future?

The key to a life of power is intimacy with God, and this starts with laying down your life and surrendering to Him. Only then can you find hope and prevail in the struggles and trials of life, and be armed with the tools that God has provided so that you can thrive on the journey. Once you light upon intimacy with God, your life will grow in fruitfulness.

I'm praying that this book will encourage you to encounter Jesus in a new and wonderful way, to draw you closer to our God and give you inspiration to walk in the love and power of God, with His immeasurable goodness and abundant mercy following you all the days of your life until you are called home to be with the Lord.

My Father, I pray that the person who is reading my words today may come to delight and trust in you more and more. That you will take them into the deep waters of your love. To open the eyes of their hearts to your goodness and grace.

That they may come to know and love you for who you are and for their hearts to beat with the rhythm of your heart. That they know the hope of your calling, the riches of the glory of your inheritance and the exceeding greatness of your power towards them when they believe.

Release your glory, Lord, so that every soul may shelter under your wings. That in that sanctuary they may find the peace that passes understanding.

May we all be awed by the incredible gift you gave us in Jesus. That we may appreciate what He did for us in His life of sacrifice and devotion.

That we all may be strengthened with all might according to His glorious power to completely and mightily accomplish all the good things our faith prompts us to do to the glory and praise of our Lord Jesus Christ.

AMEN.[1]

---

1   Psa. 37:4-5; Eph. 1:19; 2 Thess. 1:11-12; Col. 1:11.

## Chapter 1
# God Saves Me From a Cult

*"For by grace you have been saved through faith,
and that not of yourselves; it is the gift of God,
not of works, lest anyone should boast."*
**(Eph. 2:8-9)**

My journey to being saved has been a challenging journey, with all sorts of obstacles and impediments along the way, but it's a journey that I would make over and over again in a heartbeat. Grasping that we are now living in the Kingdom of God, that we are ruling as kings and priests, sitting in the heavenly realms with Christ Jesus with authority to overcome all the power of the enemy[2] has been the most rewarding, fascinating breath-taking and exciting experience I could ever have imagined.

In the lives of most Christians there has been one person or book or article that led them to hearing the Gospel. I didn't have any of these. My mind was tightly closed to reading any Christian tract or literature and I would never have listened to any Christian speaking about what they

---

[2] Luke 10:19

believed. I wouldn't even allow Christian songs to be heard in our house. God alone had to reach in, rescue me and personally re-educate me about His truths.

I grew up as a Christadelphian, a cult that was founded around 1850. Christadelphians reject the doctrine of the triune Godhead, the existence of the devil and the present possession of the Holy Spirit. They teach that Jesus was a specially created man with God as His Father. Jesus was enabled by God to live a perfect life to model to us how we should live. He died in perfect obedience to His Father and so saved Himself from the power of death.

Christadelphians teach that all those who trust in Jesus and are water baptised have joined the family of God. Jesus' death on the cross was a representative offering — not a substitutionary offering for us in our sins. Salvation was said to be dependent on having certain doctrines correctly understood together with a demonstration of works. Believers who died remained in their grave until the resurrection and thereafter were to stand before the Judgment Seat of Christ to have it determined if they would be saved or not. The saved were expected to be rewarded with immortal life on earth for 1,000 years.

It is extremely difficult to be delivered from the bondages of Christadelphian beliefs. The late Phyl Gibson, who together with her late husband, founded "Freedom in

Christ Ministries", once remarked to me that she had never encountered such a strong demonic stronghold on people's minds as she had encountered with individuals exposed to Christadelphian thinking. Furthermore, most people who, of themselves, leave the cult are hardened against Christianity and the ones I have met over the years who did leave have been left bitter and angry about their wasted years in the cult.

I want to point out, from the outset, that I believe that people with Christadelphian beliefs can be saved. My own father had been a zealous member, but he had died totally oblivious of the blessings that are to be had in Jesus' Kingdom of Heaven. Ten years after he had died I was lamenting to God that my father hadn't known the truth about Jesus and salvation by grace and straightaway the Spirit had said to me, "I am merciful. Don't you remember that as he was dying he was pointing to a person?" (Just before my father had died he had indicated, with his eyes opened wide in disbelief, that there was a person in the room with us, over near the doorway and I, thinking he was going crazy, had walked back and forth in the space he was pointing to, to show him that no one was there.) The Spirit went on, "Your father was pointing to my angel who brought him to me."

Another time the Spirit had told me that being a part of the Christadelphians was like associating with a friend of Jesus, but not Jesus Himself. Specifically the Spirit pointed me to this verse: "Tell me, O you whom I love, where you feed your flock, where you make it rest at noon. For why should I be as one who veils herself by the flocks of your companions?"³ In other words, as a member of my old religious group, I was only getting a fraction of the true picture about Jesus and for Solomon's bride, and for all seekers of truth, that simply was not good enough!

Little incidents throughout my growing up years had introduced me to the foreign concepts that God loves me, that Jesus died instead of me and that prayers from Christians actually were answered. Those early memories resulting from incidental meetings with Christians came flooding back when I finally encountered the reality of the Holy Spirit.

The first time I can ever remember actually feeling uncomfortable with the teachings of the Christadelphians was when we had a church minister publicly debating belief in the Trinity with a prominent speaker within our group. There wasn't a shadow of a doubt in my mind that the minister was going to be totally trounced in the debate, so watertight were all our arguments against the existence of the Trinity.

After the debate, as our group members went about

---

3   Song of Sol. 1:7

joyously congratulating one another on the vanquishing of our opponent on the Trinity, I was amongst them feeling utterly dismayed. Our champion had neither heard any of the minister's arguments to enable him to contradict what I then believed was the absurdity of the Trinity nor had he proffered a strong position for Jesus not being God. I felt quite ill at our inadequacy to meet the theologian's arguments and worse, I didn't know in myself how to realistically counter those arguments. For the life of me I couldn't understand how my brethren thought we had won the debate with such inadequate and paltry anti-Trinitarian arguments. Very privately, however, I was disturbed and deeply considered what that theologian had presented.

The second time I had some doubts was after I had done a personal in-depth study of Galatians. I was in my twenties when I came to the different conclusion that we are saved when we have simple faith in Jesus, not by what we do. When I aired this conclusion to group members, I was quickly brought back to the party line that faith had to be in explicit doctrines prescribed by the founder of the group accompanied by so-called "works". I bought that argument and let the idea of salvation by grace lapse until two decades later.

Although, no doubt, in looking at the cult from the outside, you would think life in the group was odd, I want you to understand that in the religious group there was a degree of security in life and the experiences weren't all negative. Life was like what I'd imagine life in a tribe would be like. We had common values and socialised frequently and easily. We received a Bible education like no other from early childhood. Apart from the rigorous home instruction and memorisation of Bible verses, we had Sunday School where, over five years, the entire Bible was carefully studied before the cycle recommenced. Like a school subject, we had homework and examinations. Yes — we had national age-delineated Sunday School exams every year, and, I might add, the exams I sat in my later teen years were far more rigorous than any exams I have ever faced in Bible Colleges.

I also learnt bits and pieces of Hebrew, Jewish songs and customs. I explored how to study the Bible and use lexical resources to analyse texts. I studied Koine Greek, which has been extremely useful to me over the years. The ability to easily reduce swathes of writing or speaking to a single paragraph or two is a skill that was acquired through the preparation of countless formal synopses throughout my teenage years. Proficiency at analysing an argument, critical thinking, debate and essay structuring all resulted from my years associated with the Christadelphians.

There was also a tight familial bond and social structure amongst the members so that we could go anywhere in the world and be received as family by members. On top of that, because marriage could only be between fellow cult members, we had actual family connections with large numbers of people. It would only take a few moments of discussion to find a common relation with anyone who has been connected to the group for some time — especially since large families were fairly common.

Life in the group was about adherence to a set of doctrines that the founding father had developed in the 19$^t$h century — all without any passion towards God or searching for any emotional connection with Him. We were encouraged to love the Bible more than loving the Author of the Bible, studying the Bible assiduously to understand it within the prescribed framework. Having the "right" doctrine was regarded as far more important than even having the right life so that people had been excommunicated or disfellowshipped over different interpretations of words.

No relationship with God was ever mentioned. I look back now and think I was actually in an Old Testament time warp with harsh and authoritarian rules without the New Testament's freedom resulting from the ministry of the Holy Spirit leading to heart-led fervent obedience to God. I erroneously believed that "hope" was "faith". (More on this in Chapter 9: "The Power of Your Faith".)

In a conversation with a Christian in the 1990s, he had pointed out that Christadelphians served God out of fear whereas Christians served God out of love. I had been most indignant at him saying this, but when I reflected on those words afterwards, I realised that he was making quite an astute observation and I was left challenged and not a little disconcerted.

Jesus was never seen as a person, a real person who died for us. Doctrinal wranglings, theological disputes, fellowship issues, attendance at activities and end time prophecies were all placed above the importance of knowing and pursuing Jesus.

As I have said before, salvation was unassured because members believed they were accepted at the Judgment Seat of Christ only by their merits — merits which were based on correctly understanding the group's interpretation of selected doctrines and practical performance (the definition of which varied widely). The gap between your theoretical and practical performance to that of Jesus' was filled by Jesus in His mercy and this was termed "grace".

As a strict Christadelphian, there was absolutely no reading of Christian literature or Bible translations other than the KJV (King James Version), listening to Christian songs or association with Christians. You have to understand that I was the third, fourth and fifth generation in my family to have been associated with that group and all I had ever known had been life in that environment. I only ever mixed with friends and relatives who were in the group and I was very much discouraged from any contact with anyone from "the world".

Christians were viewed as being of the world and were all a part of the religious system that was referred to as a harlot in Revelation. The prospect of a suitable marriage partner was limited as you could only ever be married to someone "in the Lord", a fellow Christadelphian. To marry outside of "the Truth" was to invite excommunication or "disfellowship" as it was termed and disassociation.

In my particular ecclesia, education past Year 10 was frowned upon so I continued the last two years of my high schooling under a great deal of pressure to give it all away. Surreptitiously I went on to university. Inevitably my studies did become known and I received much criticism and scorn privately and was shamed publicly for pursuing worldly wisdom. I was required to religiously attend all meetings, usually about five to six each week, including nights before gruelling university exams.

Weddings were affairs full of endless speeches about marriage and the woman's role in deferring to the husband. My own wedding, however, was a whole new level of disaster.

On my wedding day everything went wrong that could possibly go wrong. My flower-girl was so overcome with nerves after walking down the aisle that she vomited when she reached the platform. As I walked down the aisle I could see the celebrant quietly trying to mop things up with his handkerchief.

Then there was no pen to sign the wedding certificate so the celebrant hastily pulled out a fine drafting pen that he had had on him. My father-in-law pressed too hard on the thin tip when signing his name as a witness and the nib snapped and ink splattered onto the marriage certificate.

But all this was nothing compared to what happened next at the reception. It was time for the speeches and we had a man in his early sixties from NZ speaking for my ex-husband's NZ family. He managed to introduce himself and then gasped that he couldn't go on and promptly collapsed and died, right there and then, directly in front of the bridal table. Paramedics amongst the guests valiantly tried to revive him on the floor where he had fallen until the ambulance arrived. The ambulance officers took over, continuing to work on him in front of our bridal table. In the end, after what seemed like an eternity, he was carried out and pronounced dead.

And so commenced married life! Even though to an onlooker it would appear to be a strange world to live in, at this stage I wasn't questioning anything that I had been taught. I had some misgivings, as I have already explained, but I wasn't challenging anything. This was the only world I had ever known.

The very first indicator that there was something else outside of all I had ever known about God was an event that happened around 1984. I was having a conversation with an elderly lady. After about an hour of talking about work-related matters, she suddenly stopped and said, "You didn't tell me you had the Holy Spirit inside you."

I protested strongly that I didn't. I told her what I had been taught from childhood — that the Holy Spirit was only the invisible power of God, by which He had created the world. I explained that the Holy Spirit couldn't be separated from God, even as you can't separate the sun and its light, the fire and its warmth. I told her that the influence of the Holy Spirit in this day and age is only through the power of the word of God, the Bible. I wouldn't hear of her suggestion that the Holy Spirit was a person.

She was taken aback, but she didn't back off. She questioned me if I had read the Book of Acts and what had happened when people were prayed for to receive the Holy Spirit? Of course! I had read the Book of Acts many times, twice a year to be exact, almost every year of my life. (Christadelphians routinely follow a prescribed reading plan of three chapters from the Bible throughout the course of a year.)

She then asked if I had been prayed for to receive the Holy Spirit. No, I most definitely hadn't. She questioned if I had prayed on my own to receive the Holy Spirit. Never! The very idea hadn't even entered my head. I added what I had believed at the time — that possession of the Holy Spirit had ceased with the death of the last apostle.

At this point she looked at me intently. Pointing to my chest she said, "My dear, don't tell me that I'm not seeing the Holy Spirit in you. I know what I am seeing. It's as clear as I am looking at your face."

She looked confused for a while, but then added, "Well, if no one has prayed for you and you haven't prayed for the Holy Spirit, then God must be showing me this because He intends to place His Holy Spirit in you."

She wanted to pray for me then and there to receive the Holy Spirit, but I reacted like Dracula confronted by a crucifix. Her comments to me were so absurd that I dismissed the whole episode, but obviously never forgot about them.

Each night we, as a family, would read the King James Version Bible, and we would seek God's help in understanding just who God was, "no matter what the cost". It was my earnest prayer that God would reveal to me an understanding of what He required from me, that I would know His ways and serve Him acceptably. The cost was irrelevant. I sincerely wanted to do life God's way.

In my quest to understand God, He started revealing the concept of grace to me. I didn't know I was searching to understand grace, but after five years, that's where my initial searching concluded. When you've been taught to read the Bible in a certain light and there is an intricate structure that you've had instilled in you to understand grace, it is very difficult to see grace objectively or even any differently.

The search for understanding grace had become quite time consuming with every free minute taken up with pondering what had been written in the Bible. I was hungry to understand God, and the words: "A satisfied soul loathes the honeycomb, to a hungry soul every bitter thing is sweet"[4] aptly describe the hunger that I experienced in wanting to understand this concept.

It was a struggle to superficially read the verses that I had been taught to indicate that salvation was dependent on a correct doctrinal understanding.[5] I pressed on. Since the Bible clearly says to "Work out your own salvation with

---

4   Prov. 27:7
5   E.g. I Tim. 4:16: "Take heed to yourself and the doctrine. Continue in them, for in doing this you will save both yourself and those who hear you."

fear and trembling,"[6] this must mean that you need to try really hard, to strive and to agonise in order to be saved. Clearly, salvation was a work — a work that I was called upon to perform. Since we are told that faith without works was dead,[7] then I had actions that I must do to save myself. The struggle to perform at a high enough standard to be like Jesus and know that you kept on failing was soul-destroying, to say the least.

There were just so many anomalies throughout the Bible that perplexed me. It was an inconsistency, for instance, that Abraham was called a man of faith for obeying God's command to traverse wild and trackless wastelands while he was still a pagan idolater![8] I really struggled with someone being termed a man of faith before the biblical doctrines were correctly understood.

The verse, however, that finally enlightened me in my quest for understanding was: "For by grace are you saved through faith; and that not of yourselves; it is the gift of God: not of works, lest anyone should boast."[9] The verse, as it read in English, was interpreted by the group differently, but it was when I read the Koine Greek that it had been translated from, that I understood exactly what was being said here.

---

6    Phil. 2:12

7    Jas. 2:17

8    Josh. 24:2; Gen. 12:1; Heb. 11:8.

9    Eph. 2:8-9

"Saved" was a Greek word in the perfect tense and passive voice. The perfect tense in Greek is not the same as the perfect tense in English. In Greek it has the added meaning that something was done in the past and its effects were still present at the time of writing, so in a sense it is a past tense and a present tense at the same time. The passive voice indicates that the subject was acted upon by some other performer of the verb.

In other words, and struggle as I might, and no matter how many times I read and reread that verse, no matter how hard I tried to understand it from the perspective I had been brought up to believe, it was clearly saying that I had been saved in the past and was still saved in the present. I couldn't get myself saved now. It had all been done for me — I had been saved by a power outside of myself. My salvation wasn't conditional on my actions or my strict adherence to a set of made-up doctrines. Grace had saved me. Grace through faith alone. Both were gifts from God.

I had tears in my eyes when I read and finally understood that verse. My lifetime of failure and inadequacy dissipated and I knew that my Saviour had done for me what I couldn't.

I was just so delighted to read Paul's words: "The life that I now live in the flesh I live by faith in the Son of God, who loved me and gave Himself for me"[10] and realise that Paul wasn't, as I had been taught, some special person who had a divine revelation by the Holy Spirit that he had been saved. I, too, had the same blessing because Jesus had died for me, personally, and given Himself for me, personally.

There was no more fear in believing in Jesus. No more shame because I couldn't be as perfect as Jesus. No more living in guilt. No more dread of getting to the Judgment Seat to await the final verdict. I was saved now when I believed. Praise and glory to our ever merciful Father, our Saviour!

Now I understood why becoming a Christ follower is not about trying to be good. Salvation is about a radical transformation starting with complete forgiveness and acceptance in the Saviour. While we trust in Him there continues to be forgiveness and acceptance as He transforms us into His likeness.

After years of poring over my Bible God alone had showed me that Jesus was my Lord and Saviour and I was saved. That moment of sheer surprise and delight is indelibly etched on my memory. All my struggles to work for my salvation evaporated in an instant and I knew that, by believing in Jesus, I was saved. I couldn't get myself any more saved and I couldn't get myself any less saved.

---

10   Gal. 2:20

I was so excited to know that Jesus was my Saviour and that my feeble efforts were irrelevant to my salvation because He had paid the price for me to be redeemed. He had resolutely set His face towards the cross to save me from the power of death because I couldn't. To look at His overwhelming sorrow with sweat falling down like great drops of blood and know that He stayed His terrible course for me was a tremendous revelation.

I wanted to share this incredible message with all my fellow Christadelphian brethren, but there was a problem. Openly admitting that my Saviour was not a representative that I had to model my life upon and to rather say He was my substitute was regarded as unscriptural and would have been cause to have me disfellowshipped for wrong doctrine.

So I asked God for help. I asked Him to send the people who needed to hear this message. I prayed that the sign for me to share this wonderful news was for them to declare, "I don't believe I can be saved." In one week alone four group members spontaneously confessed that to me so that I could confidently share the Gospel with them and see them freed from the torment of fear.

To give you an idea of how freeing the discovery of grace is to those who were oblivious to its import, let me tell you about an incident I had at a Christadelphian nursing home. I was talking to an elderly lady from the group who confided to me that twice she had been on the verge of dying, but she had stopped herself because she was terrified of meeting Jesus at the Judgment Seat. She told me that she had been haunted with this fear her entire life and that sometimes at night she would wake up agitated and upset at what awaited her in the future.

I sat with her for an hour and took her through her Bible, reading to her the wonderful words of hope for all those who believed in Jesus, how we are totally forgiven and our sins are never brought to mind again, showing her the assurance that the saints have for salvation. I asked her if she believed in Jesus and she said that she did.

I told her that she was therefore totally forgiven and could confidently expect to be welcomed by Jesus into His Kingdom. I showed her that there was no judgment for those who believe: "He that hears My word and believes in Him who sent me has everlasting life, and shall not come into judgment, but has passed from death into life."[11] You should have seen her eyes! It really was one of the most poignant moments in my life. She hugged and thanked me with tears in her eyes and said that now she could die in peace.

The following week when I went to the nursing home she wasn't there and when I asked where she was I was told she

---

11  John 5:24

had passed away during the week. I can just imagine the joy that filled her heart when the ever grace-full Jesus called her home and she delightedly responded to His call.

That grace-full Jesus is calling out to every person on this planet. He is going to inordinate lengths to find you and rescue you from sin and death. He suffered a severe beating that could have killed Him so you didn't have to suffer with diseases. He even died instead of you so you could be saved and be called a child of God. I want to tell you more about this love.

## Chapter 2
# In Love God Seeks to Save You

*"Set me as a seal upon your heart, as a seal upon your arm; for love is as strong as death; Jealousy as cruel as the grave; its flames are flames of fire, a most vehement flame."*
**(Song of Sol. 8:6)**

*"The Spirit who dwells in us yearns jealously."*
**(Jas. 4:5)**

We had devastating bushfires in Australia at the end of 2019, and we saw acres of bushland, homes, animals, birds all being destroyed in moments of time. We saw unbelievable gale-force winds in firestorms sucking everything into the flame; and this towering inferno is what God means when He says he jealously loves those who love Him! He envelopes them in a fierce fire of passion and woe betide anyone getting between Him and His beloved. His love doesn't ebb and flow — it rages for eternity.

Our faithful Saviour loves us this much that He pursues and woos us like no other; His almighty flame of love blazes like an intense and wild fire that stops at nothing. So what does this extravagant love look like when God seeks you out? How does God pursue the unlovable?

The Bible gives us some examples of people who we would consider unlovable yet God sought to save them. Their God-dishonouring decisions, moral failures and obnoxious behaviours didn't stop them being immeasurably loved and sought by God.

Adam and Eve were living in paradise. They had delicious food to be had just for the taking, no need for protective clothing from the elements or environment. Friendly wild animals. Daily chats with a loving God. But they wanted more and threw it all away to listen to the lies that came from a serpent. So ashamed were they of turning from God they hid in the garden, but God sought them out and made a way to save not only them, but all of their progeny, all of humankind. Us.

Zaccheus was a tax-collector who was believed to have abused his position by adding a little extra to the demands on his clients, but when little Zaccheus climbed a leafy sycamore tree in order to just see Jesus, Jesus called him out from his obscured vantage point in order to save him.

After Saul had played his part in the stoning of faithful Stephen in Jerusalem, Jesus found him on the Damascus road and called him to follow Him.

When God is after you, you can't hide from God. Sin will never be too great for God to reject you. Your social ostracism won't cause God to turn His head away from chasing you. Your most disgusting behaviour towards God's people won't stop God seeing your heart and running after you.

God seeks and saves the lost and ostracised and He wants to save you and put you in His family. You are of such immeasurable value to God that He has sought you out so that you can dwell in His house forever. When Jesus looks at you, He looks in love at your glorious future.

Even when you are saved and you fail and sin, we can be sure that God is near to you and will not forsake you. David wrote that, "The steps of a good man are ordered by the LORD. And he delights in His way. Though he fall, he shall not be utterly cast down; for the LORD upholds him with His hand."[12] This means that God expects us to fail! He expects the good person to fail and sin, but He has promised to not leave us there, but He will pick us up and keep us going.

You may be thinking that Adam and Eve, Paul and Zaccheus just made poor decisions and bad judgments and you can understand how God would forgive them.

---

12   Psa. 37:23-24

Do you want to hear the shocking story of someone who sinned horrendously and was still saved? Right at the beginning of the Bible is the unbelievably sordid story of Lot, the nephew of Abraham. Practically everything that is recorded about Lot is vile and hideous yet Peter referred to him as a righteous man.

Lot chose to live in Sodom, a city of such depravity that God sent fire and brimstone against it. Lot was so engaged in the Sodom culture that he sat in a position of honour and power at the gate of the city. His wife was unquestionably attached to the culture of Sodom that she notoriously became a pillar of salt when she disobeyed the command to not turn back whilst it was being judged. Lot once had two angels visit him and the men of Sodom wanted to have homosexual sex with the angels so Lot offered the drooling wild men his two virginal daughters to be gang-raped instead. (In the goodness of God, the angels blocked that from happening.) After that his two daughters induced Lot to get drunk and had sex with him on consecutive nights and thus produced his grandchildren.

I find it difficult to understand a God who would want to save a person like that. The only good that we are told about Lot was that he hated the evil that was going on around him in Sodom. His mind was linked to the one who would make him righteous, even though his actions were quite contrary to everything we know about God and His holiness.

What does that tell you? Lot was declared righteous, not because of anything noble or good that he had done, but in spite of all the evil he had done he was saved because of what Jesus had done for him. God doesn't save you, either, because you are "nice". God saves you purely because of what Jesus has done for you.

Lot's story tells us what God is really like — when a sinner repents, God forgives them. God wipes every sin away. This explains why God didn't destroy the wicked people of Nineveh after they listened to Jonah and they repented. (If ever you are in doubt about how wicked they were, go visit the British Museum and look at the reliefs taken from the king's palace in Nineveh.)

Again, Ahab was the most wicked king in Israel's history, but when he heard through the prophet, Elijah, of God's planned judgments against him, he repented and God postponed those judgments for another generation. If God's records of forgiveness of the most evil people are recorded in the Bible, you have the full assurance that when you come to God with a repentant heart, no matter what you have done, God will forgive you.

We have access to the kingdom of God[13] when we repent and believe that Jesus has forgiven us of our sins. No matter

---
13   Mark 1:15

who you are, what you have done or where you have been, the Spirit of God is a free agent to regenerate a person when He likes, how He likes and where He likes. And what could be fairer than this — at the end of the day, no matter how long we have been serving Jesus, we will each receive the same reward.[14] With God, there is no such thing as having 144,000 witnesses grabbing the best seats on a first come, first served basis; or pushing in to claim the position on Jesus' right hand and left hand, millennia before millions of disciples had even been born.

My life story and your life story are given to us so that we can bring praise to the God of heaven who has: "Delivered us from the power of darkness and conveyed us into the kingdom of the Son of His love".[15]

The early Christians knew what God had done for them and had such an intimate relationship with Him that they joyfully sang His praises as they were burning at the stake. There are records that Nero put his fingers in his ears to drown out the sound of the Christians singing.

I want you to live with all the divine privileges, resources and blessings that are available to you in Christ,[16] standing with your shield of faith to quench all the fiery darts of the

---

14   Matt 20:2-16 (The parable of the workers in the vineyard.)
15   Col. 1:13
16   Eph. 1:3

wicked one[17] and in so doing bring all praise and thanks to the One who loved you and gave Himself up for you as a fragrant offering and sacrifice to God.[18] How do we wipe away every word we should never have said? How do we wipe away every action of guilt and pain that we are ashamed of? The answer is belief in JESUS so that no accuser can point the finger and say your guilt is there for all to see. Jesus has taken it away and that is a very good reason to praise God.

Do you want another reason to choose Jesus? Well, think about the Law of Conservation of Energy where energy cannot be created or destroyed. You exist in the present and therefore you must accept that you will exist in some form or another after your death. The form you end up in is your choice, but we have a loving God who is yearning for you to choose to spend eternity with Him.

Every person who has been saved has an amazing testimony of how God worked in their life to lead them to being saved and every single story should be told. Every single person! I love listening to people's accounts of how God reached into their lives and saved them, but I'll recount two that stand out to me for their craziness.

One was about an Australian man who used to regularly

---

17  Eph. 6:16
18  Eph. 5:2

travel to an American city to speak to the people living on the streets about a Saviour who could set them free and deliver them from being captive to a life of pain, helplessness and hopelessness. You will never read anything about him. He was the most unlikely looking character — rough, semi-literate, broken-toothed and looking very much homeless, himself, but he had a real heart for preaching Jesus to the lost.

One evening he suddenly found himself inside a brothel. He swears solemnly that he had been walking along a street waiting for God to tell him who he should witness to when the next moment he was in a place that he would never have wandered into of his own choice. He was bewildered until he heard the Lord telling him to witness to a certain young lady in there, who also happened to be naked. With his witnessing she came to repentance and in tears she knelt on the ground in front of him and he led her to the Lord. Afterwards she dressed and they both left the premises.

The other incident occurred when a young lady and her friend were working in a far north Queensland city. They were bored, and as all the venues for entertainment were shut on the Sunday night, they decided to head to a local church "just for a laugh". When the altar call went out, they headed to the front, giggling. The pastor came and prayed over the young lady and recounted her entire life to her

— facts that not a soul was aware of. In that moment she realised there really was a God in heaven and she repented and has now served Jesus for going on fifty years.

Undoubtedly, then, the power in your testimony of salvation is towards yourself, but it is also towards others. There are records of Romans in the stands who witnessed the early Christians burning at the stakes singing with joy towards their beloved Lord, and who then leapt over the barricades and ran towards the Christians, knowing that they would share their fate, but wanting to have that same closeness and intimacy with God, no matter what the cost. Even today there are people who would die to have what you have. There are people who are envious of your relationship with our Saviour. Let me relate from my own experience.

It has been my privilege to work with hundreds of people from all over the world and many of these people have come from backgrounds where to become a Christian has a huge price tag, ranging from social ostracism to death. Once I was teaching English (on a voluntary basis) to a group of about 30 people from south east Asian countries. One Thai gentleman shared that when he had accepted Christianity his entire family had disowned him. He was tearful saying how he had lost contact with everyone he had loved. Some people in the audience concurred that that's what would have happened to them, also, if they had become Christian.

At this point I shared with them that the price of me becoming Christian was to also lose contact with all my family and friends. They were incredulous that such a thing could happen in a Western culture. (My mother continued her contact with me, but she was cautioned against doing so by different ones.) I told them that ostracism was a price that I would gladly pay over and over again, such was the incredible place I now was in to know the living God. I then asked the Christians in the group to put their hands up and told them that they were more my brothers and sisters than my own flesh and blood. Something clicked at that point and a great percentage of the class wanted to become Christian. What a small price I had paid to form the catalyst to seeing so many saved! What the enemy had meant for evil, God had used for good.

I would've been happy to spend the rest of my days waiting in anticipation of living out eternity with such a Saviour, but God had more in store — I read in my Bible how He wanted to have a deep intimate relationship with me. He wanted me to be so close to Him, so trusting of His protection over me, so in love with Him that I'd snuggle up to Him like a young chicken burrowing into the feathers of its mother.[19] He wants us enraptured by His beauty, desperate for Him, wholly sold out to Him and laying our souls down for Him in every area of our lives.

---
19  Psa. 91:4

A miraculous life will continue if we surrender everything and invite the Holy Spirit to come into our lives. There was a price to pay, but the coming of the Holy Spirit into my life meant that there would never be a "normal" to refer to ever again and that thereafter would follow an adventurous life full of wonder and surprise. I will tell you more later about communion with God, but I'd like to backtrack first and give you the background to how I first received the Holy Spirit and circumstances that followed on from that.

## Chapter 3
# The Power of the Holy Spirit

> *"So I say to you, ask, and it will be given to you; seek, and you will find; knock, and it will be opened to you. For everyone who asks receives, and he who seeks finds, and to him who knocks it will be opened." … "If you, then, being evil know how to give good gifts to your children, how much more will your heavenly Father give the Holy Spirit to those who ask Him!"*
> **(Luke 11:9,13)**

A farmer's wife had told me many years before I understood anything about the Holy Spirit that in her early years of marriage they had been dirt-poor and they had had no quilts for their children. They lived in the northern NSW tablelands so the winters were bitterly cold. She had one duck, which they intended to eat, and she planned to use its feathers and down for stuffing quilts. You don't need to be Einstein to realise that one scrawny free-range duck wasn't going to make enough filling for one quilt, let alone three single quilts!

She prayed to the Holy Spirit and asked for a miracle and

God was faithful — there were enough feathers and down to fill three quilts sufficiently densely to keep her three children warm throughout the following cold winters. She even had enough feathers left over to make a feather pillow. Her husband confirmed her story and because she was so ardent I didn't doubt her veracity at all. Hearing her story, however, was very challenging at that time to my understanding of what the Holy Spirit was. As I felt the feathers in the quilts I couldn't deny a miracle had taken place.

There came a time in 1999 when I was selecting the five hymns for a Sunday morning service. By way of explanation, Christadelphians have no paid clergy — male members deliver all the talks. As the appointed visiting speaker was running late and I hadn't been able to get in touch with him beforehand to see what themes the hymns should be on, I prayed to God. As time was short I prayed that wherever the hymn book fell open, that those hymns would be suitable hymns to support the message. I have no idea what I was expecting to happen because I didn't believe that God's Holy Spirit answered prayers in this day and age, but without any more thought I hastily selected the five hymns where the hymn book had opened.

As the message unfolded, I realised that the hymns were complete mirrors to the message being given. Had I read the message fifty times I couldn't have chosen more suitable hymns. I was shaking and in tears. The opening hymn for meditation was a complete précis of the talk that was to follow. How was that possible? I knew that God could only have done that through the Holy Spirit, but I hadn't felt anything and I was severely challenged for I had been dismissive of the Holy Spirit acting on individuals like this. This was to prove to be a life-changing encounter with God for me.

As I sat there in that meeting I made a vow to God that I would explore what the Holy Spirit was, and what and how much I could ask the Holy Spirit for. I had no reference book but the Bible. I couldn't refer to books from the religious group as they rejected the Holy Spirit operating on individuals in this day and age, and the very thought of referring to Christian books was not tenable, since I believed these people did not hold the truth of the Bible. God alone had to teach me through His written word.

At this point I'm reminded of the words of the French mathematician, Blaise Pascal, who in 1670 wrote: "There is enough light for those who only desire to see, and enough obscurity for those who have a contrary disposition."[20] If you really want to know a matter, there are enough hints to whet your appetite to search ardently, but by the same token, there are enough shadows to encourage you to complacency.

---

20   http://www.leaderu.com/cyber/books/pensees/pensees-SECTION-7.html accessed 7.10.20

So with that small light shining on the power of the Holy Spirit, I set out to read my trusted KJV Bible from cover to cover to uncover this mystery. I prayed for God's help as I yielded my heart to God to reveal what had been in my Bible all along. I coloured in green every reference to the Holy Spirit. After six months of hungrily digesting my Bible from cover to cover, I sat back and looked at my now gaily decorated Bible, and came to the conclusion that when you believed in Jesus as your Lord and Saviour, you were automatically filled with the Holy Spirit.

This may sound a pretty obvious conclusion, but this was ground-breaking for me. To acknowledge this to members of the cult that I was in, would have had me quickly disfellowshipped. That was a scary thought, but I hadn't satisfied my hunger to know just what the indwelling of the Holy Spirit meant and what sort of requests I could ask of God. There still wasn't any peace of mind for me.

Interestingly, Paul said that the peace of God surpassed understanding.[21] Simply, God's peace, the gift of wholeness, far exceeds reason, faculty or intellect. It is a heart thing. It's far above the God-given capacity of a person to think. At this point, my thinking that my quest was an intellectual exercise was very wrong. I didn't know it, but I was really seeking to have the "eyes of my heart" enlightened.[22]

---

[21] Phil. 4:7
[22] Eph. 1:18

Around this time I attended the wedding of a man who I had been presenting the doctrines of the cult to. Although normally I didn't attend anything outside of the group's activities, especially in a church, the future groom had come into my office the day before his wedding and begged me, for various compelling reasons, to attend his wedding. I felt I couldn't refuse and so I attended his wedding.

As we parked our car at the wedding, a recent graduate from a Pentecostal Bible College pulled up beside us. He had travelled 460 kilometres to attend the wedding because God had told him he had to witness to someone at the wedding. He introduced himself, and, because my every minute up to this point in time had been exploring the Holy Spirit, the conversation quickly turned to the topic of the Holy Spirit. My questions started in the morning, continued all throughout the day and night until this man left after midnight.

Further, the songs sung at the wedding had lyrics that had surprised me. Because of my very strong Biblical background I recognised countless scriptural concepts and I was taken aback that a Christian could have comprehended the Bible so fully to link those concepts together and talk about a freedom or depth of knowing God that I had only recently begun to explore. (Little did I realise that, ironically, I shared relatives with this particular songwriter because he had had the same religious background to me.)

If I had had questions before, there were now far more to replace them. What I had heard from this man at the wedding about the working of the Holy Spirit had me incredulous. He was either telling me lies, was mad or he was telling the truth. Since he had a demeanour like one of my uncles and came from a rural community, I decided that I should trust him.

A few months later a strange set of God-orchestrated circumstances led me to go to a church service for the first time in my life. There "just happened to be" an altar call for people to come forward to be prayed for to receive the Holy Spirit and I felt compelled to go forward.

I went to the back of the line to be prayed for. I saw people falling to the ground and I thought that they were all being hypnotised so I shut my eyes tightly. I prayed to God and asked that if all I was hearing about the Holy Spirit was true, then please show me so definitively that I wouldn't miss it.

When the pastor came over to pray for me, he told me that he had to firstly order a demon off me before I could receive the Holy Spirit. I wasn't ready to think about the possibility of the existence of dark forces, a supernatural devil or his demons, but since I expected that this would be the only time in my life that I would ever find out the truth about what I was hearing and reading about the Holy Spirit, I said to myself, 'Whatever!' and stayed put.

The demon was commanded to leave in Jesus' name and it must've slipped away quietly because I didn't feel anything particularly. Then the pastor prayed for the Holy Spirit to come into me and I felt something that I can only describe as a heavy dense quivering cloud over my head. He prayed again and I felt myself being wrapped in a hovering pulsating presence. I was feeling very alarmed and wondered what was going to happen next.

The third time he prayed I felt something like thousands of volts of electricity painlessly surging through me and even though my eyes were shut, I saw water with light through it spurting through every part of my body. It was like the water gushing out of a garden hose when it is first turned on, but the water didn't scatter everywhere — it raced so rapidly with purpose and direction. I collapsed to the floor in a state of utter peace. It was more than peace. It was sheer delight. I couldn't move. In my mind I wanted to stay there in the presence of God forever. I found I couldn't move a muscle physically — if the building had caught on fire I couldn't have moved, even if I had wanted to.

Eventually I was helped to my feet and all I could exclaim was, "It's true. It's true." I was just incredulous. I figured then and there that since the Christadelphians had been so terribly wrong about the power of the Holy Spirit, then it stood to reason that they could be terribly wrong on almost anything else. I promised God in that moment to set about with a vengeance to find out what the truth of the Bible really was.

Just a note on the receiving of the Holy Spirit — it is different for every person, for: "The wind blows where it wishes, and you hear the sound of it, but cannot tell where it comes from and where it goes. So is everyone who is born of the Spirit."[23] The work of new birth in us is according to God's free will, we can't determine its origin or know its destination. All we know is that we cannot enter the kingdom of God unless we have been born again by the power of the Holy Spirit.

God provided me with a companion to help me along my journey of discovery. I had initially met her in a group of mothers of my youngest daughter's friends, but I met her again as the matron of honour at the wedding I had attended. I bumped into her again when I had rung a local Pentecostal church to speak anonymously to someone about all these strange events that had been happening to me and she had answered the phone and recognised my voice. She had literally been walking past the reception and the receptionist had asked her to man the phones for a couple of minutes. I bumped into her again when my youngest daughter had badgered me incessantly to take her to her friend's house for a play date during the school

---

23   John 3:8

holidays. The penny dropped at that point when I turned up at her house and saw her again and I admitted to her, "Obviously God wants us to talk!"

Well, we talked and talked on many occasions. She was knowledgeable and very helpful to my journey out of the group. She especially understood the ostracism because she had come from an Assyrian background into the Gospel light and had suffered similarly.

I was bewildered, though. I still kept thinking the Christadelphians must hold the truth of the Bible, even though they had been so wrong on the Holy Spirit. I prayed to God to understand what He thought about the group and He answered very strongly. I had several Bibles, of all shapes and sizes, but no matter which Bible I opened, with eyes opened or shut, no matter how many times I turned those Bibles around, whenever I asked God about His attitude to the Christadelphians and opened the Bible it always fell open to the very same passage: "Go, and tell this people: Keep on hearing, but do not understand; Keep on seeing, but do not perceive. Make the heart of this people dull, and their ears heavy, and shut their eyes; lest they see with their eyes, and hear with their ears, and understand with their heart, and return and be healed."[24]

---

24  Isa. 6:9-10

In those early days I was still officially a member of the Christadelphians and was strongly influenced by their thinking. I therefore thought I needed to have a correct understanding of the Bible in order to be acceptable to God. It was at this time that God gave me a dream.

I dreamt that there was an old house in the countryside that was full of household groceries that were free for the taking. Crowds of people were flowing in and grabbing as many grocery items as they could carry and scuttling off as quickly as they were able so that they might return for more. I joined the throng and while I was there clutching things I saw a door that nobody else was aware of. I cautiously opened the door and entered a huge room full of expensive items of art. I stood and marvelled at a large beautifully framed Gainsborough painting and a floodlit, magnificently intact, large decorated ancient Grecian urn on a stand. At this point I looked up and saw a young man with his back to me, sitting at a bar. I asked him if I could take these items and he replied that I could, but why would I when I could just ask his Father for far greater treasures than these?

God was gently showing me that there was a lot more to be had from greater intimacy with Him and that I should keep on pressing in. It was all very well to be searching for doctrinal truth, but there was something far greater to be had, just for the asking. I was simply being told to not stop at searching the wonderful Being of God — that knowing God will go on for an eternity, rather like the four perceptive and discerning beasts around the throne singing: "Holy, holy, holy, Lord God Almighty, Who was and is and is to come"[25] over and over and over and over forever. With each refrain they have a fresh revelation of knowing God and His holiness.

The Bible had become a living book. Verses would literally jump out at me, dancing around the page and highlighting aspects that I had previously missed. It was unbelievably exciting. I could ask questions of God and either He spoke directly to my spirit or, as I turned the Bible's pages, the answer would jump out. It was as if the verse was under a magnifying glass. I was only just beginning to find out the enormous help that is available to the believer through the Counsellor, the Holy Spirit.[26]

I was on a journey of learning to hear the voice of God and it is still my prayer that my ears will be increasingly attuned to hearing the voice of the Holy Spirit. I am not alone in that request. When Solomon became the king of Israel, God asked him what he would like to receive. Solomon replied that he was but a child and that he was in the middle of a great people so he asked, "Give to Your servant

---

25   Rev. 4:8
26   John 14:26

an understanding heart to judge Your people."[27] That word "understanding" in the Hebrew can also be translated as a "hearing heart" or a "listening heart".

But I've been recounting to you the good news — there was a flip side to all that was happening and I was quickly made aware of the bad news.

---

[27] I Kings 3:9

## Chapter 4
# The Devil Makes Himself Known

*"She has cast down many wounded, and all who were slain by her were strong men. Her house is the way to hell, descending to the chambers of death."*
**(Prov. 7:26-27)**

*"Be sober, be vigilant; because your adversary the devil walks about like a roaring lion, seeking whom he may devour. Resist him, steadfast in the faith, knowing that the same sufferings are experienced by your brotherhood in the world."*
**(I Pet. 5:8-9)**

I saw his form at the side of my bed. It had been leaning over me surreally spitting out unintelligible words in a high pitched hissing voice and now it had noiselessly glided to the rear of my bed. I assumed it was my then husband. We lived on rural acreage and had large dogs that barked at anything that moved so an intruder was most unlikely. I addressed the apparition as my husband and asked him why he was speaking so weirdly. It just stared at me and didn't answer. I asked the question again and still it didn't answer. I was confused. If it wasn't my husband then it must be Jesus. When I asked if it was Jesus it immediately vanished.

Shortly after receiving the Holy Spirit, I had been continually prompted to understand the evil one. I had no idea whatsoever of the existence of a devil: to me the idea was just a fanciful creation of someone with an overactive imagination, but here I was face to face, in my darkened room, with a dark shadow the size and shape of a man.

A couple of days later I had another weird experience. I was inside our house, which had many large windows in each room, and I saw a black raven fly and hit the glass in the window next to me. Small birds saw their reflections and would hit the panels in the windows and I thought it strange that a large bird would be bothered by its reflection in a small panel of glass. It hit the window again. I calmly went to the window to shoo it away when I saw it flying at the window yet again. It hit the window with a thud, bending its little neck right back.

I stood there waving my arms and banging the window and the raven hit the window yet again. I thought the poor bird was confused and would surely kill itself if it kept this up so I went to the other side of the house in order for it to get its bearings and go away. To my surprise it hit the window on that side of the house, also. I decided then that, for some incomprehensible reason, the bird must be attracted to me so I walked inside our indoor pantry and waited there long enough for it to fly away. I still didn't grasp the idea that the devil and his unclean and foul birds were a reality.[28]

(NB I am not suggesting at all that ravens are unclean and foul birds — just that this particular one was used by Satan to try and intimidate me. Recall the prophet, Elijah and how he was fed meat and bread by ravens at a brook in the Kerith Ravine. Ravens used to come onto my balcony twice a day for handfeeding and they were always very personable with their gentle wakeup calls. Endearingly they would turn their little heads every which way to make their glistening throat feathers stand out like an Elizabethan ruff.)

You may think it should've been easy to accept that there was a supernatural devil since I had actually seen him, but it wasn't exactly straightforward to let go of 47 years of beliefs that had been ingrained into me. The group's founder had decreed the way the Bible should be read and interpreted and it was nigh on impossible to read my old familiar Bible through impartial eyes, try as I might. Verses about the personal devil and Satan, for example, were all explicable within the definitions of the group's doctrinal structure.

I prayed for God to help me understand what the Bible had

---

28   Rev. 18:2

to say about the devil and God came back with: "It is the glory of God to conceal a matter, but the glory of kings is to search out a matter."[29] Apparently there wasn't going to be a shortcut to my understanding!

I read and read my Bible but couldn't understand the devil any differently to what I had always understood. The devil had blinded me for: "The greatest trick the devil ever pulled was convincing the world that he didn't exist."[30] Too many years of brainwashing had forever wrecked my being able to understand familiar texts in any other way. I appealed to God. I told Him that, try as I may, my old belief systems were getting in the way. I told Him that I really wanted to understand for myself what was the truth of the matter, but I knew I couldn't help being biased before I had even started.

I was eating my breakfast shortly after that when the Holy Spirit began reciting to me the Lord's Prayer, but when He arrived at the part: "Deliver me from evil", He related: "Deliver me from the evil one." I knew better than to challenge the Holy Spirit, but what was it with "evil" modifying another word? I'd always understood that "evil" in that context was a noun. I immediately reached for my arsenal of weapons — my majority text Koine Greek Bible, concordances, interlinears, lexicons, Greek

---

29  Prov. 25:2
30  Charles Baudelaire, quoted in www.shmoop.com accessed 29.2.20.

analysis books, other translations and you name it and was surprised to find that the word "evil" was in the genitive case and therefore many other translations actually put in the word that it was modifying so it would read "the evil one". It was technically more accurate to translate the Greek as, "Deliver me from the evil one." I was ever so slowly beginning to grasp that there really was an evil force in the heavenlies.

When I related to some group members about this strange apparition in my bedroom, my tale went viral and I was mocked and jeered mercilessly from all corners of the globe. I prayed to God and the Holy Spirit reminded me that Eliphaz the Temanite had had a similar experience.[31] He had had a spirit brushing his face and he, likewise, could only make out its form. Furthermore, that spirit had said to Eliphaz that God had charged the angels that had sinned.

I don't think I'd ever noticed that verse before, especially with it saying that angels could actually sin, and I hadn't realised before that the angels in Eden experientially knew good and evil, but there it was on the printed page of my Bible.

The final piece in the jigsaw came when the Holy Spirit prompted me on three separate occasions in the space of

---
31  Job 4:15-16,18

a few days to read the Book of Enoch.[32] It was in this book that God was referred to as the Lord of the spirits and I immediately realised that God was the ruler of the angels and of evil spirits. The book also explained about angels sinning, their wicked deeds and their punishment.

Now I knew who the enemy was, the attacks against me were about to become a whole lot more interesting and things were about to become much fairer. I learnt about the formidable weapons I now possessed against him and started seeing some amazing events, but I now want to tell you the good news about living under the power of the Holy Spirit.

---

32  This is what is called a pseudepigraphical work that is cited in both 1 and 2 Peter and Jude. It was an ancient book that, for various reasons, wasn't included in the canon of scripture.

## Chapter 5
# Communion with God

*"I have found David the son of Jesse, a man after My own heart, who will do all My will."*
(Acts 13:22)

It was 6:30 am and I had just heard the words sung, "When Christ shall come, with shout of acclamation, and take me home, what joy shall fill my heart. Then I shall bow, in humble adoration, and then proclaim: 'My God, how great Thou art!'" when my phone fell silent. I looked at my phone to see what was happening and saw that there was an incoming call. It was from the hospital where my mother had just been admitted.

"I'm sorry to inform you, but your mother has just passed away. Can you please come in to make arrangements?"

But God had only just told me that He had already made the arrangements and my mother was at that moment bowing before her Creator in worship. How gentle was my God to break such sad news in such a merciful way!

Communion with God can take a myriad of forms, but

it is always about having an ever-present companion who shares His very heart about Himself and about things that happen around you.

Communion is about intimacy with no limit to the subject matter — once God even told me the Hebrew word to clarify an etymological link that I was puzzling over! His voice can be audible, or it may come through something you read or hear, or in pictures, but mostly God's voice comes though other-worldly impressions on your mind. When my mind is totally still I can hear that voice most clearly. Books have been written about hearing that still, small voice so I won't go into that subject here, but I will say that hearing the voice of God takes practice, a lot of practice.

This intimate personal relationship with the Holy Spirit, a deep hungering to be in the presence of God, is something I've read about in the Bible and have heard other Christians talking about. Moses wouldn't even move forward in the wilderness unless the presence of God went with him and the people of Israel.

An example of listening to God's leading is about a man[33] who was driving along when he heard the Holy Spirit telling him to immediately cross to the other side of a

---

33   Lake, John G., *Adventures in God*, 1981, Harrison House, USA.

busy highway and to park facing the oncoming traffic. No sooner had he run the wheels of his car into the ditch on the other side of the road than he encountered a huge truck veering out of control sliding down across the entire road. Had he stayed where he had been his car would have been pushed over the cliff on that side of the road. Once past him the truck hit a rough spot in the road, righted itself and went on its way.

Communion with the Holy Spirit involves the presence of God now — a dynamic and a two way interaction. This is the real Christian experience and why Christians seek to know God's heart by pressing into the place where He lives inside of you: where His voice speaks to your heart.

At the header of this chapter I've placed David — an example of a person who communed with God on a regular basis. But why? David's name is linked with some of the biggest sins in the Bible — adultery, murder, lying, treachery, betrayal. Yet God chose to approve him and communed intimately with him.

Critically, every single time David erred he repented for violating God, His person and His nature and, importantly, David learnt from his mistakes. He was humble, trusting and teachable, like a child.[34] Sin doesn't block us from intimacy with God — we do.

After David had committed adultery with Bathsheba and had Uriah, her husband, murdered, he implored God not to take away His Holy Spirit from him.[35] David's intimacy with God was paramount in David's heart because God was his friend who he communed with. He trusted so completely in God that he knew God and God knew him and his greatest fear was losing that closeness.

It is not because we are righteous or we have surpassing Bible knowledge that God communes with us. It is the opposite! God communes with those who are humble and freely admit their guilt and wholly turn to God for their direction in life. God will turn no-one away from communion with Him when they give up believing in themselves, their pride and their ambition and come to Him with their whole heart to trust solely in Him.

Back in 2000 I was frustrated at Christians who I assumed had been having all these wonderful visions and discussions with God and they hadn't told me. It wasn't until some time later that I found that this wasn't the regular Christian experience at all and then I was dismayed that so many were ignorant of this dimension of the Christian life.

---

34  Luke 22:25-27
35  Psa. 51:11

God was showing Himself more and more to me both in breath-taking personal encounters and in communing with me. I found that the more I asked God for help with every little thing that bothered me, the more I became attuned to His voice. It is my prayer that I increasingly recognise that voice above all the chatter and noisy static that besets us every day on this earth.

The more we seek after God with all our heart, the more we will have intimate private times with Him. He promised that if we delight ourselves in Him, He would give us the desires of our heart.[36] My desire is to know God more, to live a life of abounding fruitfulness that springs from being in an intimate relationship with Him. Jesus promised just before He died that if you love Him, He would love you and physically appear in person to you.[37]

We can't think that this was a promise that we would see Him again in heaven, because the followers of Jesus were all already fully aware of that and it would have been redundant for Jesus to mention that yet again. We can't even think that this was a promise given only to His disciples who were about to see Jesus once again when they were assembled in the upper room because just before Jesus had said those words He said he was speaking to whoever

---

36  Psa. 37:4
37  John 14:21

believes in Him[38] and He had repeated that He was directly speaking to those who heeded His commandments and kept them and loved Him.[39]

This was a promise to us that we would see Jesus in person again and again. Not only were we promised that if we believed in Him we would do greater works than He did[40] but we have also been promised that Jesus would make Himself visible to us. Jesus would reveal or show Himself to us. So what does this look like? I can only speak from my personal experience. Unlike others I know, I haven't seen Jesus personally, but I have seen, heard and felt His Holy Spirit.

There was a night when I was in communion with God — I was raising questions to Him in my mind and He was answering them through my mind. We were conversing, one with the other, and my whole body was quivering with His presence and my eyelids were fluttering uncontrollably. To this day I can't believe that I asked this, but I dared to ask to see God. Immediately my whole body started to shake. My eyes grew hotter and hotter until they felt like red-hot ingots of molten steel (my Newcastle roots are showing here!) and I feared that my eyeballs would melt or shrivel up, so intense was the heat. This incredibly

---

38 John 14:10
39 John 14:21
40 John 14:12

fear-engendering experience lasted for what seemed like an eternity before the heat gradually died down and I apprehensively opened my eyes. I was more than relieved to find that I still had eyes and could see. The experience profoundly affected me and abruptly brought me to an end of thinking I had anything to offer God. If we want to be used by God, then we have to yield entirely to Him, giving up our thoughts, our abilities and rely solely on God for leading and favour. I can no longer live for my desires, but for His; to live totally submerged in the river of life, His Spirit.

That first Christian song I ever listened to referred to rising from waters deep, and there is no limit to how deep we can tread into the waters of the Holy Spirit. Just like Ezekiel, we are invited by God to walk into ankle deep water, then into knee deep water, then into waist deep water[41] and then right into the river itself. Think about that! I live near the beach and I watch children frolicking in ankle deep water or even knee deep water, and they are very much in control, but get them into anything deeper than waist deep water and they are very much more respectful of what the water is doing. They watch for rips. They don't take their eyes off the waves.

God is wanting us to let go of standing in our own strength and letting Him take control of our lives. He wants us to

---

41   Ezek. 47:3-4

leave the "things of the land" at the shore and to let the "things of the Spirit" be all that matter to us.

Once I was thirsty and as I put my arm out for a drink at a Christian women's conference, I saw a huge wave coming towards me from across the table. The wave was like water with light through it and you could see crests on the wave as it surged rapidly towards me, but none of the wave crests broke away or splashed. The wave hit me with an incredible force and I went reeling backwards and crashed onto the ground in the midst of all these lovely ladies sipping politely on their cups of tea. Here was my own personal message from the Father to let Him take over my life, to be engulfed by all of Him and to go deeper and deeper into the life of the Spirit.

The Father was giving me the same message that Jesus gave the woman of Samaria when Jesus was thirsty and had asked her for a drink. Jesus had told her that whoever drank that water from the well would become thirsty again, but He could offer living water so that a person would never be thirsty again.[42] God offers all who are thirsty the invitation to be fully immersed in His love and His glory, to drink deeply of His living water and go into deeper and deeper places in His Spirit.

Throughout the Bible we find that people of God had

---

42   John 4:10,13

overwhelming experiences like this, leading them into deeper places with God. Joshua met the Captain of the host of God. This meeting made all the difference to his life. Isaiah saw God high and lifted up and prepared him for future service. Paul was lifted up to the third heaven and so profound was the experience that he was unable to verbalise about it, but it powered him for a ministry that shook the Gentile world.

Life with God is just one amazing event after another. There was a time I was praying in a group and as I prayed I found myself racing though space at a phenomenal speed. I could see planets and stars whizzing past me. When I stopped speaking, the movement stopped, but when I opened my mouth again to speak my journey resumed.

I was having many visions such as seeing the Holy Spirit falling on people like lightning coming to them at a 45 degree angle or the cloud of the Holy Spirit hovering over gatherings to consider the Bible or miniscule droplets of light-filled water falling slowly to the earth. And then there were meetings with people who the Spirit was directing me to minister to.

I was in a line-up and the woman in front of me in the queue had just arrived from interstate. She lamented that she didn't know anybody and had no relatives in Australia because her father had come from Germany just after World War 2 and her mother had been disowned by her family. It turned out that her mother had been disfellowshipped from the Christadelphians for marrying a "non-believer", even though he had been a Christian. She had therefore had no association whatsoever with her relatives as they were all in the cult. What are the chances? From there on we had an interesting conversation about what it had meant for her mother to leave the group and to become a Christian. She left with a new respect for her mother, who she had told me she hadn't seen as particularly brave before I had spoken with her. She also heard what a fabulous choice it is to choose Jesus!

Another time I was standing outside a shop and the Holy Spirit prompted me to go and talk to a woman who was standing a bit further away. I thought, I'm happy to talk, but I need an opening, Lord! As I stepped near her I heard her young son singing a Christian song, so I simply opened with, "So you are a Christian?" The woman was quite curt with me and responded, "No way! Why on earth would you ask that?" Not a good start, Lord, I thought! I replied that her son was singing a Christian song and I therefore assumed that she was a Christian. I then received a tirade about her not being a Christian, and no desire to ever be a Christian and how her mother was the one who paid to send her children to a Christian school. I told her how much God loved her, what He had done for her and the plans He had for her. She started to become teary and told me,

"Now I know that God is real. You used exactly the same expressions and words that my mother had said to me this very morning!"

I've heard of a couple in northern Queensland who spend three hours in prayer together each day and then go to the local shopping centre to listen to God directing them to people He wants them to witness to. They have many amazing testimonies of salvation.

God doesn't always prompt you to speak to people. Sometimes He will just give you words in a conversation that will reach a person's heart. That has happened to me a lot. For example, I met the mother of one of my children's friends and in the course of the ordinary conversation she told me that her husband for years had been doing workshops on astral travel. (Astral travel is an out of body experience where the soul separates from the body so that it can wander about.) I asked her, if from the moment he had been involved in those courses, had they had relationship problems, financial difficulties and sickness?

We were at a large gathering and she let out a wail and ran off sobbing loudly. I felt awkward. I certainly didn't say that to distress her and I had only just met her, too. She returned about an hour later and apologised and explained that it had been true — that for the time since her husband had been involved in these courses, they had been in severe financial distress, she and her husband were at loggerheads and that, most distressingly, her hair was falling out in handfuls and she was wearing head coverings to conceal the bald patches. Not only that, she had spent thousands on doctors and psychologists trying to get to the root of the problem, all without any relief. She had asked her minister for advice and still had had no answers. She had arrived at the point that she didn't want to recount her problems to another soul ever again and only that morning had prayed to God to send someone to her that day to tell her what the problem was and the solution. Here I was, the answer to her prayer!

I explained to her that the devil only comes to kill, steal and destroy[43] and that if you play around with any of the "devil's toys", like astral travel, there will always be a price to pay. The devil isn't particularly kind to people who come within his sphere of influence, and he is especially vicious to people who profess to be Christians. Until you address the root of the problem and get rid of demonic influences in your life, you will continue to be afflicted by demons.

There are all kinds of bondages to Satan when you mess around in his world, and there are too many people with spirits on them that make them fearful, suicidal, depressed,

---

43  John 10:10

angry, obsessive or mad, to name just a few examples. I prayed with her and ordered the evil spirit to leave in the name of Jesus and advised her to get a spirit-filled person to go through her house and identify any areas that would allow the devil to get a foothold (such as images, crystals or ornaments that have demonic connotations, like statues of Buddha) and to pray around her house and declare the territory as belonging to Jesus. Above all, she needed to get her husband free of his association with the devil — away from his involvement in the dark and sinister world of Satan.

At other times, the Holy Spirit will tell you exactly what to say. I once had a Jehovah's Witness at my door wanting to tell me about Charles Taze Russell's bizarre take on the Bible. The Holy Spirit told me to only talk about disfellowship and not talk about anything else, so that's exactly what I did. I told him that Jehovah's Witnesses couldn't hold the truth because they disfellowshipped people and that Jesus was about inclusivity, not exclusivity. He wanted me to look at the doctrines of the group, not the practices, but I insisted that by their deeds you would know them[44] and that clearly they were a false belief system because of this practice alone.

He was persistent, but I was relentless, matching everything he claimed about the so-called Jehovah's Witness' 'truth'

---

44   Matt. 7:16

with scripture about the gospel of Jesus and His inclusivity for all sinners who would come to Him and repent. There was nowhere for this man to turn. The truth of what has been written about Jesus cannot be refuted.

After an hour of this seemingly pointless arguing, he suddenly went quiet and put his head down and told me something very close to his heart. He had been a practising Jehovah's Witness but had been a drunkard thirty years earlier in an overseas country. While he was at work one day, the Jehovah's Witnesses had taken his wife and children and all their possessions and he had never seen them again. He had actually been disfellowshipped and had suffered lifelong emotional pain as a result. This poor man had been so bound by Satan — his life had been destroyed yet he wanted to valiantly share what he thought was the gospel, regardless. I was able to talk to him about a Jesus who loved him, warts and all, who had died in his place so that he could be declared righteous. This was indeed the Jesus he had been searching for, his heart's desire.

I seem to attract people who are running away from God and it's incredible but true that God, on many occasions, has seated those hurting and broken souls next to me on plane trips around the world. Even when I had a travelling companion and had booked seats together, I would find myself separated on the plane to sit next to the person God needed me to talk to, to bring them back to Him. I count it as an enormous privilege that God would use me for such opportunities to spread the Gospel.

On one occasion a man was seated next to me on a flight from Anchorage to Seattle. The Holy Spirit informed me that he had been hiding from God and was facing a life-threatening operation. When I told him this he had tears in his eyes and nodded his head. I told him that God was giving him this last opportunity to return to Him and I went on to tell him that God wanted to save him because God loved him so much that even if he had been the only person on earth, Jesus would have died for him. He protested his unworthiness and I insisted to him that God had His arms wide open for the worst of sinners who wanted to come to Him. There is nothing that can separate us from the love of God. He had his head down and nodded his head in agreement, thanked me and said that he had a lot that he needed to say to God and wanted to pray on his own. What a merciful God we serve!

Another lady I was sitting next to on the way to Adelaide was having an adulterous affair and was on her way to meet her lover. She didn't tell me any of that, of course, but the Holy Spirit impressed that on me. I talked to her about her relationship with God, how she was running away from Him and she agreed, but said she was powerless, at that moment, to return to God. She insisted she would return, but it wasn't convenient at that time. I pointed out that it had never been a "convenient" time for Jesus to die on a cross to take all of our sins, but He had willingly erased the debts and charges against us and nailed them all to the cross.[45] She didn't want to hear any more — she was in the tight grip of Satan. I pray that she did eventually get free of his control.

The Holy Spirit will challenge you way beyond your abilities. I had just completed an Auslan course, the language for communicating with deaf people in Australia. To say I was a poor student is putting it mildly, but at the time I was able to converse in general chit-chat. I had been sitting in Sydney Airport heading to Adelaide, with the flight being repeatedly delayed when I noticed two deaf people struggling to understand what was happening with the flight on the departures board. Being unable to hear the PA announcements, they were sitting there totally bewildered. I went over to the couple, explained I was a hearing person and could I help them? When I explained about the flight delay I suddenly found myself surrounded by about thirty deaf people plying me with question after question and getting me to speak on their mobiles to relatives who would be concerned about their no-show in Adelaide.

After that had been dealt with, they explained that they were all Jehovah's Witnesses and had just attended a

---

[45] Col. 2:14

conference in Sydney. I started debating with them about the meaning of Abraham being justified by his belief in God and his demonstration of that trust in God by actions that God had specifically requested he perform to demonstrate his assurance in God[46] — not by works of his own choosing to earn his salvation. My point was that actions were directly demanded of believers in random ways by God in varying contexts that would directly demonstrate that person's confidence in God in contrast to Jehovah's Witnesses who believe that they must log the hours that they publicly witness each week in order to be saved. God never decreed that a man-made rule of subservience to an arbitrary rule was acceptable to Him and would earn their salvation.

I had thirty proficient Auslan speakers overwhelming me with comments and arguments from every direction. I was seriously out of my depth, but somehow God gave me the grace to be able to witness to some of them and reveal the awesome plan of God to save us by grace, and not by works. I'm convinced that God calls us out of our comfort zones to be His witnesses here on this earth and that he will use us where we are, with whatever skills we have and that all God wants is a willing heart.

However, whenever you are witnessing about Jesus there

---

46   James 2:21

will be attacks by Satan. Frequently these attacks come through other people, like when Peter rebuked Jesus for Jesus saying He was heading to Jerusalem to die there. These attacks from other people hurt the most, as I was about to find out.

## Chapter 6
# Evicted From the Cult

> *"Blessed are you when men hate you, and when they exclude you, and revile you, and cast out your name as evil, for the Son of Man's sake. Rejoice in that day and leap for joy! For indeed your reward is great in heaven, for in like manner did their fathers do to the prophets."*
>
> **(Luke 6:22-23)**

I had been bringing in the washing from the clothesline when I heard a car coming up our long driveway. It was being driven by the Recorder, or Secretary, to our particular Christadelphian ecclesia. With a serious face he handed me a letter that said I was being formally disfellowshipped from the group's worldwide community because I believed that the critical doctrine for salvation was belief in Jesus as your Saviour, that the Holy Spirit was available today and because I associated with Christians.

I've referred to the fear of being disfellowshipped from the group that I had been born into. This is a fear that besets every member in the group because it spells withdrawal from everything that you have ever known and every person you have ever associated with. In my case, probably about 20 per cent of the Australians in this cult were my relatives, as my roots in this group went far and wide after the conversion of so many of my forebears.

With my talking about these new-found beliefs it was inevitable that I would be swiftly removed from the group, but I wasn't prepared for how brutally that process would be enacted throughout all the different assemblies. Many people who have left this group of their own accord have been left broken and unable to make headway with their lives, but when Jesus leads you out of darkness, He provides all the support and love imaginable.

The Secretary from one particular assembly rang me one morning, and with no discussion whatsoever informed me that, until I recanted, I was to neither set foot in their hall nor was I ever to speak to any of their members again. I was instructed to give their members a wide berth if ever I was to accidentally come across them. The no-contact rule was also announced to their members at their Sunday morning meeting. It was as if I was a super-spreader of COVID-19!

Feeling so utterly rejected and abandoned by all my friends and family, I shed tears the whole day. I kept hearing: "Leap for joy" over and over and over again. I was too busy feeling sorry for myself to listen, though. In the late afternoon I finally started to settle and pondered what was being said to me all day long — this "Leap for joy". It turned out that God had been directing me to the quote I have at the top of this chapter. God understood that I was being excluded and rejected for His name and had been trying to comfort me the whole day long and I had been far too self-absorbed to listen. What a gracious heavenly Father we have who weeps when we weep and who comforts us when we sorrow! Not to mention what esteemed company I had in my suffering!

Another time the Holy Spirit came and comforted me was when I heard vicious and hurtful lies being spread far and wide about me in the group. It's one thing to have people shouting at you across a shopping mall that you have "lost your salvation", or making fun of what you said, or shunning you on the street and actively avoiding associating with you ever again, but it is quite another thing to have shameful lies being said about you. I appealed to God and straightaway God replied, "Who do you think is the father of lies?" God was of course referring to the words of Jesus[47] and was informing me that the devil was behind all the lies that were busily circulating. These people from the group, because they had absolutely no concept of the existence of a supernatural being that hated them, had no defence against his attacks and played easily into his hands.

---

47   John 8:44

Satan is the slanderer who does not hesitate to slaughter reputations.

Members of another assembly from the group contacted us to have a meeting to convince us to return. They were sincere and didn't want to lose us. It would have been a simple matter to just repent of what had been said and then quietly resume our seat at the rear of a meeting again. I prayed to God for help. I really was at sixes and sevens. I actually asked God to send someone to advise me on what to do. My prayer went something like: "Don't send any Christadelphian or Pentecostal that I know — these people all have agendas and both sides are biased and will want us. Send someone tomorrow to speak to me — someone I have never met to tell me what I should do. If you have sent them to tell me to leave the group, get them to say, 'You're on the right track. Don't turn back. Keep going on the path you're on.'"

What are the chances of some totally random stranger saying all of that the next day? About 2.30 pm an elderly lady rang on a long distance call to speak with my daughter. My daughter only had met this woman once and had discussed a few things with her and the old lady wanted to check up on her. I told the sweet old lady that my daughter was at work and I would get her to ring her back. She then said in a quivery strongly Australian-accented voice, "Before I go, I just want to say, "You're on the right track.

Don't turn back. Keep going on the path you're on." She had to ask me if I was still there on the other end of the line. I was in tears. I finally stammered out to her what I had prayed the previous evening and she replied, "Ohh. I just love it when God uses me like this!"

The very first Sunday morning service I went to in a local Pentecostal church after the disfellowship, I had walked in feeling like a pariah. All my friends and most family members had disowned me. In public I was being abused and shouted at on a regular basis. My children had received horrible treatment from their former friends. My youngest, who attended a school managed by the cult, was told by one of her classmates that they didn't have to be nice to her any more because her parents had been disfellowshipped. And they weren't. She had her hair pulled, was tormented and ostracised from social activities outside of class time to such an extent that, despite the school's management trying to control the situation, I had to withdraw her from the school.

So feeling outcast and unwanted, I rather cautiously walked into a Pentecostal church one Sunday morning where I was immediately hugged and welcomed. I don't know if I had looked scared and frightened, but I was taken aback by such warmth and asked if they really wanted me and the pastor who was welcoming people replied, "Want you? We've been praying for you to come!" Ever since that moment, my association in churches has been nothing but welcoming and positive with unconditional love like I never had experienced before.

God continues to draw people from cultural or religious communities that, in embracing Christianity, they must sever all contact with their own blood relatives. Some pay even more dearly with their lives. When I heard recently of a group who had been disfellowshipped from the same religious group I had been a part of, I knew the price they were paying for choosing to follow Jesus. I shed happy-sad tears for them. I was happy for their courage and the adventure they were embarking on with God, but I was sad for their losses in terms of family and associations.

So true are the words "Where no oxen are, the trough is clean; But much increase comes by the strength of an ox."[48] If we don't press in to God, if we sit around complacently and do nothing, there will be stability, order and tidiness in our lives, but when we set our shoulder to the plough and press in to know God, there will inevitably be upheavals and prices to pay, but there will be enormous blessings.

Even though I had been ousted from my family and friends in my old religious community and was attending a Pentecostal church, I was still grappling with the extent

---

[48] Prov. 14:4

of God's love for me and I had a lot of doctrinal baggage remaining that needed to be amended. God then arranged for me to be in a learning environment.

In the course of time, I had been asked by my first church to establish a K-12 school. Establishing a school is relatively easy, a matter of looking at what is required and meeting the legislation, regulations and standards, but establishing a Christian school had me feeling very inadequate. I enrolled in a post graduate course on Christian education so that I could get an understanding of how I should frame the structure of the school.

Apart from having access to a comprehensive library that I just devoured, the course included theology units, and, of particular interest, a unit on the Old Testament. I was already well-familiar with the Old Testament, but there was a slant on the Old Testament that I hadn't specifically studied — the presence of Jesus throughout every book and chapter of the Old Testament. With my indwelling divine commentator speaking to me as I read, I started to appreciate Jesus in a way that I had never seen Him before.

I remember so many times being in awe at the magnitude of who Jesus really was. He truly was the Word made flesh! He had physically been there all throughout the Old Testament. The Holy Spirit was showing me appearances of Jesus that I have never heard anyone refer to. I think this was probably the singularly most exciting part of my journey of discovery about Jesus and led me into a deep appreciation of the interplay between God the Father, Jesus the Son and the Holy Spirit — the Greek περιχώρησις (perichoresis) — a harmonious relationship of love with mutual giving and receiving.

From then on, life in the Spirit was becoming even more exciting. There was even more to be revealed. God led me into researching the Bible to discover the amazing truth of His healing power over sickness and emotional pain and then to apply that and see that God miraculously heals. God's word was true, is true and will be true forever.

## Chapter 7
# Discovering that Jesus Heals Today

*"If you listen carefully to the LORD YOUR GOD and do what is right in His eyes, if you pay attention to His commands and keep all His decrees, I will not bring on you any of the diseases I brought on the Egyptians, for I am the LORD, who heals you."*
**(Ex 15:26)**

"No?" I queried. "Please let me pray for your back. It's not something impossible. All I want to do is ask God to heal you."

"No. Do not even think of praying for me."

I had bumped into an old friend from the cult in a local shopping centre and he was bent over with back pain. He was adamant that he didn't want any of my prayers for him and his debilitating and crippling ailment.

That was an understandable response from a member of

the cult. I had started out in life not having a skerrick of faith. I even believed that it was my efforts that would get me approved by God. I had absolutely no idea about who Jesus really was and what His mission on earth had actually been so it had been up to God to lead me on an adventure of discovery to understand more about Him and what He had done for those who believe in Him.

There was a time about 16 years ago when I was prompted by the Holy Spirit to research the name "Jesus". The Latin name "Jesus" is derived from two Greek words: "ie" and "sous" (from "sozo"), which literally means "God saves", "God heals" or "God makes whole." I will elaborate more on what I found in Chapter 15, but, in short, the Greek word "sozo" was used throughout the New Testament for literal healing of diseases and the metaphorical healing from sins.

The more I read through my Bible, then, the more I saw that healing from sins and healing from diseases were commonly put together. In fact, when Israel left Egypt on their way to the Promised Land, God revealed who He was to them with one of His covenant names — Yahweh Rapha or "The Lord that heals". Israel had passed safely through the Red Sea and the Egyptian army pursuing them had been destroyed. They had been physically saved from certain death by Egyptian swords. They were travelling through a dry wilderness and found a body of water at Mara that wasn't drinkable. The short story is that God healed that water and promised them to be their God who would heal them.

This wonderful promise must've been accepted by each of the three million or so Israelites because we are told later: "He brought them out with silver and gold, and there was none feeble among His tribes."[49] Imagine all those people, old men and women, pregnant and nursing mothers, toddlers and babies and not one of them was ever sick. What's more, they were always ready to travel another day through the inhospitable wilderness. No wonder that the people dwelling in the lands they passed through were frightened witless of them.

Just a note: This Hebrew word "raphe", "to heal", is rather like the Greek word, "sozo". It appears nearly 70 times and every time it appears it means to "restore", "heal", "cure", or "a physician". It is used in both the physical sense and in a moral and spiritual sense.

It is my desire, in writing this book, to have you fully understand what being "saved" means and the blessings that have come to us through Jesus: the power to forgive you of all your sins, the power to heal all shame and guilt and the effects of sin: sickness and death. To be clear, though, the greatest movement of power that we can

---
49  Psa. 105:37 KJV

experience in the short interval that we have been given on earth will always be the transformation of a person's soul from darkness to light.

The healing of the soul is without parallel in its import in the eternal scheme of things. There is miracle after miracle of healing recorded in the gospels and Acts, but physical healing was only incidental to God's chief mission — the healing of people's souls. Jesus' mission statement starts with being anointed to preach the gospel and set people at liberty. Whilst sickness and disease are readily obvious physical expressions of being entangled and bound, what really troubles humankind is the dark and sinister disease lurking deep in our souls — the disease of sin.

There are countless illustrations of healing in the Old Testament and these incidents always point us to Jesus, our Healer — an entire book could be written about healing in the Old Testament and Jesus alone. The theme of God saving us, saving us from our sins together with saving us from our diseases, goes right through the Bible, from Genesis to Revelation. As much as God wants to heal a person's soul, He wants to heal a person's body and His promises are clearly written throughout the Old Testament. The healing of the body is proof that God has the power to heal the soul.

Notice how many times Jesus said to those He healed, "Go and sin no more!" or "Your sins are forgiven." Or when the Pharisees chided Him for sitting down with sinners, He retorted, "Those who are well have no need of a physician, but those who are sick" [50] and that He came not to call the righteous but the sinners to repentance.

Whilst He went about healing people, Jesus was ever inviting the people to "Come to Me, all you who labor and are heavy laden, and I will give you rest. Take my yoke upon you and learn from Me, for I am gentle and lowly in heart, and you will find rest for your souls."[51] Healing from the burden of sin was the reason that Jesus came into this world. If Jesus came to forgive people of their sins, but He also healed people of their diseases, then, by pure logic, Jesus must be doing both of those things today.

As frequently as we see people saved and healed from all their sin and shame, we should be seeing people healed of diseases. Healing from diseases must be the proof that Jesus heals us from our sins. We can't see that we are saved from our sins, we accept that by faith. When we accept by faith that we are healed from our diseases, then we will see physical healing take place and that physical healing is proof to us that we are spiritually healed.

---

50   Matt. 9:12-13
51   Matt. 11:28-29

My understanding went up a few notches when I heard a visiting preacher from Adelaide in a local church about 18 years ago. I believed God healed, but I didn't believe in God healing diseases that had been present from birth. I had come in late to a meeting and was standing at the rear of a large crowd when the visiting preacher pulled me out of that crowd and said God wanted to heal my blood disorder. No person on earth knew or even cared that I had a blood disorder from birth except my GP and me! My transferrin was only ever three-fifths saturated despite the presence of free-floating ferritin. In other words, I had more than sufficient iron in my blood, but the transporter was just not picking it up and taking it around my body. This resulted in me suffering from anaemia all my life — anaemia that became severe enough to require me to receive blood transfusions, iron injections, double doses of iron tablets, to have a diet geared to increasing my iron absorption and to be hospitalised a couple of times. After that unsolicited prayer, however, I have never had the problem again — my transferrin has always been fully saturated and my iron readings have since been at the upper end of normal.

After being so graciously enlightened there was no limit to what I believed God would heal and I started praying for people to be healed and began seeing that Jesus did in fact miraculously heal today, just as He had 2,000 years ago. I think the first person I prayed for was a non-believer, a man in his sixties, hospitalised with osteomyelitis of the ribcage. He was wracked with pain and he had been told that it would take time to isolate the germ causing the infection and after that it would take nine months until the medications could get through his body into the bones.

I prayed as much beforehand that he would allow me to pray for him as I did for God to answer my prayer for his healing. When I arrived at the hospital, he was groaning in pain and was surprisingly receptive to me praying for him. After my short visit I left. By the time I had arrived in the carpark the nuclear medicine team had arrived at his bedside and explained to him that he had definitely come in with this infection, but the images taken that morning showed no trace of the infection and he was promptly discharged. (Note: We had been praying for him to become a Christian and from that moment he commenced praying to God and eventually became a committed Christian.)

After that we had a friend who had borrowed our tractor and slasher. It had tipped and thrown him under the slasher and he had heard his bones snapping like twigs breaking. After a trip to the local rural hospital and x-rays, he was shown where his leg had been broken in five places. Being the weekend he was bandaged, given crutches and told to return to the hospital on Monday for the specialist to work on him. On Sunday about three of us prayed for his healing at church and on Monday, when he fronted at the hospital, the very same x-rays showed no breakages whatsoever.

Right on cue the devil stepped in to try and destroy that growing belief in the power we have available for God to heal. My doctor gave me an electrocardiogram and after three tests it consistently showed a short PR interval. He gravely told me that I could drop dead at any moment and sent me to a cardiologist to have it reviewed pronto. I left the surgery and I remember walking across a large park and laughing out loud to Satan — "Thank you for giving me a good story, Satan. I'm not being healed from a stubbed toe — I have a real testimony!"

Of course I prayed to Jesus for a healing and totally expected there to be nothing to worry about. After 24 hours of wearing a halter monitor, there wasn't anything exciting for the cardiologist to review and he wondered aloud about why I had been even sent to him.

But Satan wasn't finished with me, yet. He wanted to really intimidate me so he pulled out his big guns — the C word.

## Chapter 8
# The Diagnosis of Cancer

*"At evening, when the sun had set, they brought to Him all who were sick and those who were demon-possessed … Then He healed many who were sick with various diseases, and cast out many demons: and He did not allow the demons to speak, because they knew Him."*
(Mark 1:32-34)

"Kris, what's up?" asked Pete, when I rang him from work.

"I've been asked to come back for a closer review after my recent mammogram," I replied.

"When do you have to go?"

"I've rung them and I'm going tomorrow. Can you come with me?"

'Sure. Don't stress, though. It's probably nothing. I've heard about people who were recalled and it was nothing."

"Yeah. I'll be fine."

"No matter what happens, God is in control."

Following a routine mammogram in April, 2019 and a further four hours of intense investigation I was found to have two lumps in a breast and at least one lymph node with cancerous cells that had to be removed. Initially that's the only place they thought the cancer had metastasised to — it was only later that I discovered how wrong they were with the cancer scattered all over my lungs. The breast surgeon talked about the different surgical options including a full mastectomy. Such a shocking turn of events and so out-of-the-blue.

I was too busy for this. I had been responding to questions following a punishing two day educational institution audit with the government regulator and here I was hearing that I may not even be around in six months!

The surgeon informed me that I'd be put on fairly intense chemo so that I would be nine months fighting for my life and, on what he thought was a more cheerful note, that I should make it so that I could possibly live for eighteen months. He had put it as nicely and gently as he could, but facts are facts. There wasn't a shred of anything positive in any of that. There was no hope. He had given me a death sentence — and a death sentence following on from a long gruelling ordeal, the "fight of my life" as he had termed it.

I've known people who opted for no treatment when they had received a one way diagnosis like that.

My beliefs about healing were certainly being put to the test when I received that diagnosis of incurable aggressive metastatic breast cancer, which, if untreated, left me with six months to live. Could I really trust in Jesus to heal me and believe that it is God's will for us to be in full health and for our soul to prosper?[52]

Those early days were brutal. Let's face it — receiving a diagnosis of terminal breast cancer was a scary, confusing and distressing time. I was in shock with this diagnosis and felt like I must be on some crazy nightmare ride. My head was spinning with information about the endless tests, treatment schedules and options that lay in front of me.

Breast cancer was the very last thing I thought I'd ever have wrong with me. All my assumptions about breast cancer were debunked in one fell swoop. No family breast cancer history did not protect me. A vegetarian organic diet for much of my life, and therefore a low saturated fat intake, was no safeguard. Being told at my regular mammograms that I had the breast tissue of a young woman had given me a false sense of security. Breastfeeding for more than nine

---

52   3 John:2

years didn't shield me from getting breast cancer. I had given birth to my first child at a young age. I hardly drank any alcohol. What on earth was going on?

Whatever the cause was irrelevant. I now had a diagnosis and my only hope was my reliance on Jesus healing me. I was fully familiar with what was written about Jesus in the Bible and His healings, and I was already conversant with all the texts throughout the entire Bible about healing. From that point on I wanted to focus on my Saviour for a full healing.

I am the sort of person who will listen to a doctor's prognosis and believe it or even read or listen to anecdotes from patients and imagine myself on the same journey. I knew that about myself so I went to inordinate lengths to avoid negative tales and let what the doctors were saying pretty well go right over my head. I only superficially read the endless reports I was receiving. Even though I'm a researcher by nature, I controlled myself, when I finally knew the type of cancer I had, to just researching if there was a genetic component to it that may be relevant to my four daughters. (Fortunately there wasn't any record of genetic transmission.) I didn't need to know about life expectancies or patient experiences. I just needed to turn off my researching and thinking mind and look to Jesus.

I required an environment of faith building not faith

destroying words and thoughts. For this reason, I also didn't tell many people about my diagnosis and no one was told the full extent of my miserable prognosis. Pete, my fiancé, was the only person who knew the actual facts as he had been with me every step of the way and I could trust him because, as a Pentecostal pastor, for years he had been actively involved in faithful prayer for healings.

In fact, if I told anyone that I had cancer, I always told them that I believed that God was going to miraculously heal me. Some people scoffed and told me to face the facts, but I always told them to just wait and see. I told people that I had a God who could heal and that I trusted in Him to deliver. I spent more time telling people about God and His might than I did talking about my cancer.

My closest friends only heard the facts about what I had been told a full year later and they were saddened that I hadn't trusted them with the full story from the outset. Even if I had told my friends and family the facts and asked them to trust in the power of God to heal, it would have been nigh on impossible for them not to believe I was going to die! Their lives didn't depend on absolute trust in God and understandably they would have only had the facts of my diagnosis to trust in and would have been kindly offering me sympathy. If I was grappling with myself to believe, how much harder would it have been for them and the very last thing I needed was sympathy as I was in the fight of my life! On that point, the first surgeon had spoken truly.

David taught us that once we commit our way to God, as we trust in Him, and "feed on His faithfulness", He works. He exhorts us to rest in the Lord and be silent and wait patiently. As we delight ourselves in God, He'll give us the desires of our heart.[53] Since we had prayed for God to heal me, any talk about being sick would not have been trusting in God to heal. It is impatience and want of faith that speaks about the sickness and its symptoms and God can't operate in an atmosphere that lacks trust. Being silent about my prognosis and waiting for God is exactly what David is telling us to do.

I took sick leave as my days became inundated with tests and medical visits, but as far as anyone was concerned, I just had a cancerous breast lump that had to be removed and I was going to have treatment. I didn't want the devil's attack on me to be aired into the atmosphere where it could grow in momentum. The last thing I wanted to hear was any accusation that I had trusted in God and why had God delivered me up to cancer?

If I had heeded and believed the prognosis I had been given, then I would have been giving it pre-eminence

---

53   Psa. 37:3-7

above what God had written in His word about healing. I would have essentially been placing a curse upon myself so I deliberately played the whole diagnosis down, even asking people not to visit me while in hospital receiving treatment. The less I focussed on myself the more I could focus on God's words.

If ever there was a time in my life it was now when I needed to strengthen my faith, and I needed to do that quickly. This is what the trying of your faith is all about. Your faith is tried every time you are under pressure and you are tested about whether your course in life will stay true to what you profess.

I professed that Jesus was my Healer. I had a life-threatening disease. I could either capitulate and let the disease run its course or I could deny that the disease had any power over me because Jesus had taken every disease known to humankind when He had been beaten. Put simply, my faith in Jesus to heal was being tested, but read on to discover how I went about life from this point on.

# Chapter 9
# The Power of Your Faith

*"I have been crucified with Christ; it is no longer I who live, but Christ lives in me; and the life which I now live in the flesh I live by faith in the Son of God, who loved me and gave Himself for me."*
**(Gal 2:20)**

The following morning after the diagnosis I went to work where I told everyone that I had cancer and that I was going to be healed and that my healing would be proof to them all that Jesus heals in this day and age. Because I worked beside many traditional Chinese, the response to my news was a little different. People started tip-toeing around me, speaking to me in hushed tones and I was being plied with endless Chinese rice yogurt drinks, food and gifts. In short, I felt like I was attending my own wake.

Quite clearly, my Chinese colleagues were all saying farewell to me without having any idea of how serious my cancer was or how treatable. Just the mention of the C word in traditional Chinese culture is a one way street. I wasn't about to have any of that! I shrugged off any talk of the cancer being terminal. I recognised talk like that as being from the devil and he wasn't about to get the upper hand over my life.

I regularly told the devil, quite firmly, that he had no place in my life, to get his hands off and quit trying to wear me down with this negative talk, in Jesus' name. It was probably for the best that I quickly escaped this pervasive fatalistic philosophy in my workplace and took months of sick leave to focus on believing for a healing from Jesus.

What I was doing was a principle found right throughout Scripture, that we call things that are not as though they are. This is what faith is and this is how we are taught to operate in faith.

Let's illustrate with a look at the sobering parable of the ten virgins. Five were admitted into the marriage feast, but five were turned away. Five had enough oil for their lamps and five had insufficient oil to last the long wait. To all intents and purposes they all looked the same. For a long while they were all waiting patiently with their lamps trimmed to burn slowly, but only five possessed faith to be ready for the arrival of the bridegroom and five only professed faith to be ready.

The ten virgins parable was a parable about the Kingdom

of Heaven. They represent the Christians we see around us. All have knowledge of Jesus and salvation and all are waiting for the return of their Saviour and Lord. They are all reading the same Bible, singing the same worship songs, doing the same good works, giving money and praying. Five had a personal relationship with Jesus, did the will of Jesus, were filled with the Holy Spirit and were pressing in for more from the Holy Spirit. Five were zealous about their relationship with Jesus.

The other five didn't actually know Jesus and didn't live with the resources of the Holy Spirit in their lives. The foolish five had hope but no unyielding conviction. No wonder the bridegroom said He didn't know them. If you like, you can think about it as head knowledge versus heart knowledge. They all had head knowledge but only five had heart knowledge.

Every Christian believes they have dependence on God — that is why they are called a Christian, after all, but knowing who Jesus is, what His plans for people are, what His promises are and hoping for that to happen is not faith. It is hope. Sarah had waited for years for Isaac to be conceived right until she was past childbearing age at 90. She had been childless for 70 years That wasn't fleeting and transient hope. She saw herself having a baby every single day of those long years she spent waiting because we are told that she judged God faithful to His promise.[54]

Similarly, I knew God had promised healing in the Bible. There are copious scriptures in the Old and New Testaments about that reality. I saw myself healed every single day after the moment I was first told that I had cancer. Straight away I started thanking God for everything I was grateful for in my life and for my healing. In my mind's eye I could see Jesus standing beside me with his hand outstretched to heal me. I visualised the cancer shrivelling away as Jesus touched me. I breathed in the salt air at our nearby beach and pictured it being sent from God to destroy all the rogue cancer cells and I praised God. I felt the sun heating my body with life-giving energy that zapped all the cancer cells and I thanked God. Not for a minute did I believe that God was leaving that cancer in my body. I saw it leaving every minute of every day and I thanked God for the wonderful healing over and over again. In other words, I was living by faith and not by sight.[55]

Faith isn't knowledge about something. Trust and belief involve an intimate relationship of reliance in the heart with the One who has given us great and precious promises. When God makes a promise, we know that He will keep that promise. Paul talks about it as opening the eyes to

---

54 Heb. 11:11
55 2 Cor. 5:7

the heart to what God has assured us. It is only from the heart that we can know and love God and believe what He has pledged for us in the Bible. Head knowledge needs to be overtaken by heart knowledge if we want to be in close communion with God.

Faith is up to you. It is your choice. There were twelve spies who searched out the Promised Land under Moses. They all travelled the same roads, saw the same things, but ten said it was impossible to conquer the land. Only two spoke through their assurance in God that they should go at once and claim the land.[56] Ten looked at the problem. Two looked at the promises of God, believed them and saw the possibility.

Paul says that: "Faith is the substance of things hoped for, the evidence of things not seen."[57] In the Greek, the verb, "is" is right at the start of the sentence meaning Paul is wanting to emphasise the fact that certain conviction for God's promises is right here and now. Hope is always for a future event, but certitude in those promises is something happening in the present time. If you like, we "faith" something for here and now and we "hope" something for the future. Right now, if you are walking in faith, you are believing something good has as good as happened. Firmness in your confidence contends for the thing promised until it becomes a reality.

---

[56] Num. 13:30
[57] Heb. 11:1

I wasn't hoping for a healing. I knew that I knew that I knew I would be healed. I so much wanted that healing now that I even started to speak as if it had already happened. When my PA had wanted to mollycoddle me I castigated her and told her I was fine, that Jesus was healing me. I kept telling people that I believed in Jesus' power to heal and that they would see that He is more powerful than any cancer that can come against the body. My work colleague told me afterwards that he had never seen anyone so convicted about the power of Jesus to heal and that I had left no room whatsoever for the possibility that I may not be healed.

I told well-wishers not to worry about my cancer. I told them it was going to go, in Jesus' name. I generally received the response, "I hope so!" but that didn't stop me insisting on the fact that it was going to happen. So many people would say that they liked my positive outlook and I always clarified that it wasn't in my power to be positive or to think I was going to be healed — it was only in the power of the name of Jesus.

After I was healed, people have frequently remarked to me that it was just the power of positive thinking. I've never heard of positive thinking removing every trace of advanced cancer overnight and I've read quite a few articles and books on this and over 40 years I have met and conversed at length with some remarkable cancer survivors with positive outlooks for healing, but they all had had long protracted battles before eventually becoming cancer free. I've also met the most positive thinking cancer survivor, a remarkable young man with brain cancer. He had investigated the leading cancer research laboratories and therapies of the world and against the odds he had battled his cancer into remission time and time again, but, unfortunately, he eventually succumbed to the disease.

Unwavering reliance and trust in our Saviour is the motivator in our lives to make us a new person in Jesus. This confidence is the portal through which Jesus can manifest His power to save or heal. Boldness in your belief comes when you let Jesus' words abide in you, by being intimately involved in Jesus and doing what He says and living by everything that Jesus is,[58] so that you can ask whatever you will and it will be done for you.[59] If you don't abide in Jesus you can do nothing.[60]

Faith is the substance. It is solid. It is evidence. The certainty of your belief produces evidence. The more you know God the more you will see the results of your assurance.

I guess people think they have to actually do something in order to be saved or healed because that's the effort and

---
[58] "The just shall live by faith." Hab. 2:4; Rom. 1:17; Gal. 3:11; Heb. 10:38.
[59] John 15:7
[60] John 15:5

reward system that we are familiar with in our culture. It's also how things were in the Old Testament, but things changed when the Old Testament (or covenant) was superseded by the New Testament. In the Old Testament people were under the Law of Moses and it was by their works that they were made righteous. "Moses writes about the righteousness which is of the law, 'The man who does those things shall live by them.'"[61] In the New Testament we come under the Law of Christ, which is also called the "law of faith". "Where is boasting then? It is excluded. By what law? Of works? No, but by the law of faith."[62] We are made righteous, under the New Covenant, by the law of faith.

In other words, there's been a complete backflip under the new relationship between mortal people and God mediated by Jesus and you can only be saved or made whole from your sins by this total dependence on God.[63] Likewise, you can only be saved or made whole from your diseases by the certitude of trust in Jesus.[64] You can't continually bemoan the fact that you are a sinner and then declare that you believe that Jesus has taken your sins away. You can't work hard at being holy and hope that that will save you. You can only be saved when you have belief that you are saved through the work of Jesus. "If you confess with your mouth

---

61 Rom. 10:5
62 Rom. 3:27
63 Eph. 2:8-9
64 Acts 14:9

the Lord Jesus and believe in your heart that God raised Him from the dead, you will be saved."[65]

Once you are saved you are declared righteous. You believe that with total acceptance even though you still continue to sin, you believe that Jesus' sacrifice will cover you for all time.[66] Similarly, you can't bemoan your disease and then expect to see a healing. You can't complain or wallow in self-pity and expect you will be healed. You need to call things that are not by what comes out of your mouth and demonstrate that by your actions. That's what Jesus did and it is what we are to do if we want to see a healing.

Not once did I complain about any part of my cancer treatment process (and, by the same token, nothing happened, either, that I did need to complain!) I treated it all as part of a journey for Jesus to be glorified. I thanked God every step of the way for the way He was caring for me and providing me my healing.

Only when our hearts operate in the law of faith, when we really believe every truth written in the Bible, can the promises written in the Bible happen. Just confessing that you believe what the scripture says about something isn't applying unshakeable confidence. Praying in hope that you will be healed is not boldness of conviction. We all need

---

65   Rom. 10:9
66   Rom. 7:22-8:2

hope because that is what trust and belief is attached to; it is the assurance for faith to be convicted, but that total dependence on God needs to be developed and that can only happen when God's word comes to you.

Confident conviction is praying and seeing in the Spirit those things that are promised in the Word. "Therefore I say to you, whatever things you ask when you pray, believe that you receive them, and you will have them."[67] This means that you must speak as though you have received what you prayed for! This is such a simple principle that so many miss it. Firmness of trust is taking something that doesn't exist in the physical realm and declaring that it exists and saying, "I am healed" or "I've grasped it." If you can't do that you haven't comprehended faith.

Let me show you what I mean. When Jesus went to the wedding in Cana of Galilee, they ran out of wine. Jesus told the servants to fill the large stone water-pots used for washing with water. Jesus knew it was water that they filled them with. Peter and John knew it was water. The servants knew it was water. But Jesus called it wine and told the servants to go and draw some out and give it to the governor at the feast. Jesus was calling something that was not as though it was. He was speaking from confidence in God.

---

67  Mark 11:24

You think that was just a one-off incident? What about the ten lepers that met Jesus as He was on His way to Jerusalem? They were covered in leprosy when Jesus told them to go and show themselves to the priests to prove they were healed. As they started on their way they were still covered in leprous sores, but as they went they were indeed healed. Jesus called them healed before they actually were!

Another incident? What about the woman bent over and Jesus told her that she was loosed from her infirmity? She was still bent over when He said that, but Jesus had called for a miracle and it happened as He had said.

What about Lazarus? When Jesus received the message that Lazarus was sick, He said that this sickness was not leading to death, but to the glory of God, that God may be glorified thereby. But hang on, before we go any further, Lazarus was about to die and Jesus knew that.

Jesus knew He was dead when He said to His disciples that Lazarus was only sleeping. The disciples didn't get that Jesus was speaking in certainty of belief — they were still learning the principle that you call things that aren't as though they are, so they questioned Him about bothering to go if Lazarus was going to recover anyway. It was only then that Jesus told them that Lazarus had actually died.

Jesus had been speaking about the end of the matter, that God would be glorified in the raising of Lazarus. It wasn't God's will that Lazarus should get sick or die, otherwise Jesus would have been acting against the will of His Father when He raised Him from the dead. No, Jesus was destroying the works of Satan[68] as He was born to do. Even as Lazarus lay dead in the tomb, Jesus again spoke words of assurance to Martha that Lazarus would rise again.

Jesus told the mourners around the tomb to just believe so that they would see the glory of God. I think it would've been easier to believe if you could see Jesus standing right there beside you telling you to believe, but this is exactly what Jesus wants us to do when we turn to Him in faith. We know from what is revealed in the Bible, but also from the tangible presence of the indwelling Holy Spirit, that Jesus is ever present and we know He hears our prayers. He is right beside us telling us to just believe. "The Helper (Comforter, Advocate, Intercessor — Counsellor, Strengthener, Standby), the Holy Spirit, whom the Father will send in My name (in My place, to represent Me and act on My behalf), He will teach you all things, and He will help you remember everything that I have told you."[69]

Jesus was modelling how we are to stand on our trust in

---

68   1 John 3:8
69   John 14:26 (Amplified Bible)

God. Even in His prayer to God at the tomb, he thanked God for hearing Him. He thanked God in anticipation. Lazarus was still inside the tomb and Jesus spoke nothing but words of conviction. This is how we are to ask for a healing, with no doubts in our heart.

When Jesus called out to Lazarus, Lazarus was as dead as a dodo. Think what boldness of belief that would take to publicly name a person who had been dead for four days and ask him to walk out of their grave! I imagine the disciples must have been flummoxed by His speaking to Lazarus. Again, Jesus was calling things that were not as though they were.

What about Jairus's daughter who died? The paid mourners were outside making a commotion and Jesus told them to go away because the girl was only sleeping. They laughed at Jesus scornfully for it's impossible for unredeemed people to grasp how God works. The mourners and Jesus all knew the girl was dead yet Jesus called things that were not as though they were.

I could add more examples of how Jesus demonstrated faith to His disciples so that miracles occurred, but I'll leave it here. I just want you to understand that Jesus has given every believing disciple that same power and authority to do the same works that He did. "Most assuredly, I say to you, He who believes in Me, the works that I do he will do also; and greater works than these will he do, because I go to My Father."[70] God has already placed His healing power within us so that it is under our authority. It isn't up to God who receives healing — it is up to us.

Christianity started with miracles and it is propagated with miracles. God brought about miracles all the way through the Old Testament, beginning with Abraham believing God for an heir. God responded to their bold and active conviction and He responds in just the same way today to our audacious declarations and wholehearted trust.

While I am going to focus on healing from sickness, this same principle of faithful reliance will carry through for everything you pray to God about — such as healing relationships, finances or for people to be saved. I hope that this book can enlarge your vision and increase your confidence to see how God's power can operate in your lives.

Whatever your situation is, no matter how absolutely hopeless it looks, understand that the unending power of God is available to save you from whatever trial you are in. Any pain. Any suffering. Any shame and guilt. Any iniquities. Any sin. Any emotional upset. Any disturbance to your peace. All you have to do to access this power is

---

[70] John 14:12

to believe in the power of the Holy Spirit. Let me repeat a story[71] to explain what I mean.

During the course of World War II three missionaries riding on the back of mules had gone to the Wallamo Province in the south-west of Ethiopia. It took them three years to learn the language and another year to get to know the natives before the Italians invaded Ethiopia and drove them out leaving behind a group of 35 native Christians and a crude translation of the Gospel of John.

Five years later one of the missionaries was allowed to revisit Ethiopia and when he arrived at the Wallamo Province he found a church with more than 10,000 members. Furthermore, there were entire villages of born-again Christians scattered throughout the province, but most surprising of all were the numbers of amazing testimonies of healings — the blind were able to see, cripples could now walk.

It appears that when the Gospel of John had been translated and the missionaries had been forced to leave in such a hurry, they hadn't had time to tell the natives that the day of miracles was past and that the power of the Holy Spirit was not available today. Those new Christians had read the

---

71  Kuhlman, Kathryn, *God Can Do It Again*, Prentice-Hall, 1969, pp 137-138.

gospel as it had been written, believed and prayed and God had answered their prayers.

Time and again I have heard from missionaries how people with simple conviction have access to the power of the Holy Spirit. One missionary to India recounted to me how lepers were instantly healed, the blind could see, the deaf could hear and limbs regrew, right in front of his eyes. Another woman I know lived in the highlands of Papua New Guinea for 32 years and she told me how that several times she witnessed stillborn babies being brought back to life. In one critical incident where the village chief's firstborn son had been stillborn after a long and difficult labour, she took the baby, went off into the fields and entreated God for the baby's life for several hours. The entire village that they were witnessing to were watching and she resolutely refused to stop asking God for the child's life. With dozens of onlookers she held the baby up in the air in her hands and called aloud to God and everyone witnessed God answering her prayer and the baby coming to life.

God will bring you back from captivity: from heartache, despair, mental and physical sickness because He has plans for you — "plans to prosper you and not to harm you, plans to give you hope and a future."[72] He has given us all the answers in Christ — "For no matter how many promises

---

[72] Jer. 29:11 (NIV)

God has made, they are 'Yes' in Christ."[73] I pray this book will encourage you to dare to believe that God can deliver you from whatever your problem may be.

The enemy loves to make us fearful, stressed and worried. He loves to have us feeling abandoned, friendless and helpless. Don't let the devil's lies determine the way you think.

We have the narrative in the Bible of the small kingdom of Judah, under the poor leadership of King Ahaz, hearing of an imminent fierce attack by their enemies, the combined forces of the northern kingdom of Israel with Aram. The Bible tells us that the hearts of Ahaz and the people were shaking, just like the trees in the forest are shaken by the wind.[74] (Incidentally, we still use that idiom in English today when we say that we are "trembling like a leaf".)

God then directed Isaiah to take his son and go and meet Ahaz and tell him to be careful, keep calm and not to be afraid because the attack was just not going to happen. He told Ahaz through Isaiah that, "It will not take place. It will not happen. If you do not stand firm in your faith, you will not stand at all."[75]

---

[73] 2 Cor. 1:20 (NIV)
[74] Isa. 7:2
[75] Isa. 7:7, 9 (NIV)

Here is the key to acting in faith. We don't look at the circumstances, regardless of how overwhelming they may appear, we keep calm and believe that what has been written in the Bible about Jesus being our Healer is true and that God will not allow the evil to overwhelm us. We read, "Trust in the LORD with all your heart, and lean not on your own understanding."[76] In other words, don't look at how bad things are, just trust in God. Paul also talked about the importance of standing firm after you have put on the whole armour of God with the shield of faith, helmet of salvation, sword of the Spirit and prayer: "And having done all, to stand."[77]

Faith requires us to do something. We can't quietly sit back and wait for it to happen. Peter was told by Jesus to go and catch a fish so that the coin found in its mouth would pay their taxes. If we want to believe God for a healing, then we have to demonstrate something that confirms our belief.

It's one thing to declare that we are standing firm, but our ongoing actions will declare the level of our faith. In my case, I refused to talk about the full extent of my prognosis so some of my immediate family members couldn't believe that I had even had cancer, let alone an aggressive life-threatening cancer. If my oncologist was incredulous that there was now no sign of the cancer, it was perfectly

---
[76] Prov. 3:5-6
[77] Eph. 6:13

understandable that my own family, who hadn't been informed of the entire picture, would struggle with the whole experience.

When you want a healing from God, you need to act out of your faith. We have the example of the woman with an issue of blood who pressed through the crowds to touch the hem of Jesus' garment. Her faith had moved an impartation of power and her whole being was charged with healing power from Jesus and her weakness left her. If you can believe like this, the victory is yours.

There are two people in the gospels who received messages of what was going to happen in the future. Both were in implausible situations for the promises from God. One didn't believe, they had no faith and the other did, and demonstrated faith. The angel came to Zacharias and told him that his wife, Elisabeth, would have a son. Zacharias argued that he was old and so was Elisabeth and the angel rebuked him and told him that because he hadn't believed, he would be unable to speak until all these things had happened.

When the angel came to Mary, however, and told her that she, being unmarried, was going to have a baby, she believed and said, "Behold the maidservant of the Lord! Let it be to me according to your word."[78] Elisabeth commended her

---

78 Luke 1:38

for her acceptance of what God had decreed through the angel and said, "Blessed is she who believed, for there will be a fulfilment of those things which were told her from the Lord."[79] God wants us to be like that, too. He wants us to lay hold of what has been promised to us in His word and hold God to His word and declare that He will do it.

We can go a step further, now, in expressing our firmness in what God has promised. If we believe that Jesus is in us, and that Jesus heals today, then we can believe that the living Christ will be made real through us to every person that we lay our hands on for healing. I know, because I stepped out of my comfort zone and started praying for people with all sorts of maladies and I started seeing the power of Jesus to heal — non-Christians and Christians alike.

Too often Christians pray for someone to be healed and then add, sotto voce, "If it is God's will." They say they believe that God can heal and then add their doubts as to whether He will or won't. Just two days ago, a friend with newly diagnosed cancer told me that if Jesus wants to take her now she was happy, or if He chose to take her in 20 years' time she'd be happy — it was all up to Jesus and she wasn't going to interfere. All I could think was I was happy she didn't take that hit or miss approach to her own salvation.

---

[79] Luke 1:45

Some people state that it's spiritually juvenile to say that God heals as a reward for the quality or even the quantity of their faith. They say that this view puts too much weight on a person's ability to believe for a healing and devalues the sovereignty of God to heal as he may choose. They think that this is subtly or overtly manipulating God to perform according to our demands. These people haven't clarity about the faith that Jesus commended in the parable with the persistent bothering that the woman exhibited towards the unrighteous judge.

Jesus actually wants us to know what we want and to keep on demanding that of the Father. Just like the woman expected results from the unrighteous judge, we are to expect results from our righteous judge. Faith is persistence in belief that Jesus will do as he has promised — "All things are possible to him who believes." Visualise that small Australian lady in the highlands of New Guinea who held that stillborn baby up outside in the hot sun for hours on end and how she told God that she wasn't going to stop until he gave life to that baby and you go and act in the same way.

Why is it that in third world countries we see far more miracles than we see in the affluent, comfortable West? Is it because they know they are in need and have no other option but to turn to Jesus? Are they desperate and hungry for God and in their laid-down humility, God meets their needs? God, after all, promised to lift up the humble and fill them with good things. I think that the clue to seeing healings is to pray as though you are desperate, there is no other option, Jesus is the only answer, and then to not give up praying until you see the change you are praying for.

When I first became a Christian, I was told to just pray for people to be healed and not be attached to the outcome. Most people weren't healed, but there were some marvellous miraculous healings that were undoubtedly an answer to prayer. It would have been easy to have given up praying for people, but we need to remember that it is not about us — it's all about Jesus. If we just stay focussed on Him it won't matter what we think or what is happening around us.

Not everyone who is prayed for is healed, but we don't know if there has been some obstacle like a lack of faith and pessimism towards being healed, or a belief that sickness is the judgment of God or some human barrier like resentment, jealousy or unconfessed sin. I do know, however, that some Christians unwittingly hinder the work of the Holy Spirit. I do know that there can be no permanent victory in the lives of Christians unless they have a crystal clear understanding of how Satan was stripped of all His power on the cross so that he has no power over us. I had a personal painful encounter with such powerless Christian thinking.

My very dear friend was diagnosed quite out of the blue

with late stage metastatic pancreatic cancer that was inoperable. Given only a few months to live, she elected to have no intervention as she was told that there was nothing that could cure her and that the medicines that could be given to give her another five months would make her feel sick. She reasoned that since she was going to die anyway, then it was better to get it over and done with as quickly and painlessly as possible rather than prolong the agony and be miserable. Under the unwelcome circumstances, the sooner she was with Jesus, the better.

I sat with her and we talked about what the Bible says about healing, how God heals in this day and age and we talked about testimony after testimony. We prayed and I really felt that she believed that she would be healed, but she was to encounter an obstruction — her church's "pastoral team for cancer". Like the ancient serpent in Eden, the challenge from the team went out against the word of God with the words, "Did God really say: 'By my stripes you are healed?'"[80]

Their program of unbelief began with telling her to accept that not everyone gets healed. Then they told her that she had to expect pain because she had cancer. To make matters even worse the pastoral team became increasingly judgmental and legalistic about the terms and conditions for her being healed over the four months that followed.

---

80  Isa. 53:5

The more I told my friend to "Only believe,"[81] Jesus' words to Jairus, the ruler of the synagogue, when he had been told that his daughter was dead, the more the pastoral team voiced hindrances to her. I will spare you the details, but I was full of angst at these well-meaning Christians who were unwittingly obstructing my friend's healing and at the same time turning her children away from Jesus.

It has been said that "On the battlefield the real enemy is fear and not the bayonet and the bullet."[82] In our battle against Satan for our health, finances or relationships, it is overcoming our fear and living in faith that leads to victory. In my friend's case, it was fear that was inherent in the pastoral team that held them back from overcoming Satan and claiming back what he was attempting to steal.

Fear is an emotion that can spread rapidly and it takes huge courage to stand against it. That resolution and boldness can only come if you are convicted to your core about who Jesus is and what he did for you. Fear blocks a lot of things including love, forgiveness and intimacy, but in terms of your healing, it blocks your faith. Not even Jesus could heal people if there wasn't faith present to be healed.

---

81  Mark 5:36
82  Robert Jackson cited in http://kingdomservants.com/militarybattlewar-conflictoffense-defensesports/ accessed 12.10.20

Jesus couldn't heal people in His own hometown because of their unbelief.[83] When Jesus went to the home of the synagogue leader, He firstly threw all the mourners out of the room where the dead girl was.[84] If there is any distrust present, then the power of Jesus generally could not be manifested. Obviously this fact impressed the apostles because they repeated that Jesus was not honoured in Galilee so He didn't do miracles there.[85]

I suppose that Jesus didn't even pray for faith-less people because He had prescience about the state of their hearts. He knew that they didn't have faith to be healed. Unless the Holy Spirit has revealed to us the state of a person's belief for healing, we will pray and may not see healing.

The disciples didn't possess this divine intuition to determine unbelief on one occasion and Jesus stepped in to help them. The disciples, who had been successfully dealing with demons and sicknesses, were most surprised that they were unable to cast the demon out of a demon-possessed boy with epilepsy. Clearly the disciples had the faith to believe for healing, but the father didn't and his lack of belief blocked the healing. When the father brought the boy to Jesus, Jesus' first response was an indignant rebuke at the unbelieving generation and

---

[83] Mark 6:4-6 (NLT)
[84] Mark 5:40
[85] In Matt. 13:58 and John 4:44.

how much longer did He have to bear with them?[86] Jesus reveals to the father that all things are possible to him who believes.[87]

A further point on that incident is that Jesus taught His disciples that the key to successfully managing stubborn demons was prayer and fasting.[88] In other words, don't give up when the healing isn't immediately evident, take responsibility and find out why the healing didn't eventuate by seeking God's direction on the matter through fasting and calling out to God.

It is even more common in this day and age for people to refuse to believe in the power of Jesus to heal. I once was praying for a boy who was brain damaged from a difficult birth. As I prayed, the father said to me, "I don't believe he will get better." I couldn't believe my ears and sadly, the father received what he believed for.

Jesus didn't choose to heal every person who was suffering. When He went to the Pool of Bethesda, He only healed one paralytic even though there were ailing people all around the pool.[89] God is sovereign and He chooses who, when and

---

86  Matt. 11:16-17
87  Mark 9:14-29.
88  Matt. 17:21
89  John 5:1-15

where He wishes to heal just as much as He chooses who He wishes to save.

The case of Paul praying thrice for the thorn in the flesh to be removed is frequently cited as proof that God doesn't always heal when He is asked to.[90] For a start, there is nowhere in the Bible that says Paul was asking for a healing. I've read many theologians building their arguments on straw men and then stabbing in the dark at what disease Paul was supposed to have had. Some theologians even like to state that Paul had bad eyes because he stated that he wrote large letters with his own hand. They overlook the fact that Paul was actually saying he personally wrote lengthy epistles (which is what it actually says in the Greek).

Then I've heard some people argue that because Christians offered to pluck out their eyes for him, there must have been something wrong with his eyes, but they forget the context that the people had earlier generously wanted to give him even the shirt off their own backs, even up to giving him their own eyes, and Paul is asking what happened to them that they now regarded him as an enemy?[91] I might add that I've heard people use a similar figure of speech in saying they'd give their right arm or eyeteeth for someone.

Before we go on we need to clear up Jesus' response to Paul

---

90   2 Cor. 12:8
91   Gal. 4:15-16

about the thorn in the flesh. Too many times I've heard Christians saying that Jesus left him high and dry and told him to suffer. Nothing could be further from the truth! We know Paul prayed twice and didn't get an answer, but on the third time, Jesus met his faith and told him, "Paul, My grace is sufficient for you."[92] Paul was purely being told that Jesus would cover him with grace, or God's willingness, as much as he wanted, to take away the thorn in the flesh or anything else that bothered him, but Paul had to act on that grace.

It is when we are weak, that His power can be perfected. When we give up all effort on our part and admit our weakness and draw from Jesus' grace, then, and only then, can Jesus step in to manifest His power and meet our needs.

It wasn't sickness, either, that was bothering Paul. It was a 'messenger of Satan' that was buffeting him and causing "Infirmities (weaknesses), reproaches, necessities, persecutions and distresses."[93] God wasn't simply going to remove the thorn — Paul had to resist the devil himself and this he did because we later read that "Paul dwelt two whole years in his own rented house, and received all who came in to him, preaching the kingdom of God and teaching the things which concern the Lord Jesus Christ with all confidence, no man forbidding him."[94]

---

92  2 Cor. 12:9
93  2 Cor. 12:10
94  Acts 28:30-31

Jesus, as the word made flesh, invariably has an Old Testament scenario in His mind when He speaks and if we can find the background to Jesus' expressions, we get an understanding of why Jesus said what He did. In this case I believe His mind was in Isaiah 40 with the Gospel of comfort being promised to those who had been in warfare (verse 2). Our nature is as the grass that withers (verses 6-7), but Jesus, the shepherd, will gather His lambs and carry them in His bosom (verse 11). It ends with verses 29-31: "He gives power to the weak, and to those who have no might He increases strength. Even the youths shall faint and be weary, and the young men shall utterly fall: but those who wait on the LORD shall renew their strength; they shall mount up with wings like eagles, they shall run and not be weary, they shall walk, and not faint." Jesus sees us for who we are in all our weakness and has promised to carry us if we trust in Him totally so that in Him we will be strong. James puts the same thing in another way, "Submit to God. Resist the devil and he will flee from you."[95]

About 40 years ago the Holy Spirit was making me aware of this principle of admitting your weakness to God so that He can then strengthen you for His purposes. I composed a hymn based on how God selected judges to deliver Israel in the Book of Judges. Faithless Israel had fallen into idolatry and sin resulting in them being afflicted by their

---

95   James 4:7

surrounding nations. Inevitably the oppression led to them calling out to God in their distress to deliver them.

Every time they pleaded for help, God sent a deliverer or judge who had nothing but faith against the enemy. One was left-handed, one was a woman, one was in hiding and frightened witless, one kept on falling in love with the wrong women, one made a reckless vow, but God used those men and women who had unwavering faith in Him.

The simple and succinct message in that hymn is just as relevant to understanding weakness and trusting in Jesus to deliver. Just as He did then, He does now. Nothing we achieve can be in our own power — every victory that we have over our sins or over our sicknesses can only be accomplished through the power of Jesus who makes the weak strong.

> 1. By might and pow'r did Yahweh lead
> Israel into their land,
> But they had yet to learn and heed
> That God was their right hand.
> 2. When Israel was oppressed by foe
> And cried aloud to Thee
> Thou sent deliverers to show
> That thou alone could free.
> 3. Each judge had nought but faith in Thee
> And in Thy strength did go

> Subdued the host for all to see
> And Thy great name to know.
> 4. In lowly form Thy Son so meek
> Freed all oppressed by sin
> And we who are but flesh and weak
> In Thy strength life will win.

We have what we ask for and we have not if we ask not.[96] If we don't believe God will give us something we won't even think to ask it from God. It doesn't depend on your own worth, value, talent or even how hard you try to do something — it depends on your total reliance on God for your request. The more you pray a faithful prayer for you or others to get well, whilst forgetting about yourself and focussing solely on the Healer, the more you will see miracles.

At this point I would like to recount two incidents in the life of a pastor friend to demonstrate the principle of relinquishing everything about yourself and placing all your focus on God. He belongs to a denomination that doesn't allow for miraculous healing in this day and age. They believe in praying for the sick, yes, but healing is all "according to God's will". What happened to him filled him with awe and wonder.

He was in another room during a sermon one Sunday when

---

96  James 4:2

the speaker suddenly went silent. He waited and waited for the speaker to resume, but when nothing happened he went into the other room to find out what was happening. He found a man collapsed unconscious on the floor and everyone gathering around wondering what to do. He immediately fell on his hands and knees beside the man and prayed for his health to be restored. The man regained consciousness and his wife escorted him home. The pastor found out later that the man had been in a diabetic coma. At the time the pastor hadn't any idea of what was wrong, but he just believed that God was in charge and asked for His help and God answered that faith.

On another occasion one of his congregation had a son who had been left a quadriplegic in a motorbike accident. The mother kept imploring the pastor to come and pray for her son in the hospital so that he could walk again. He was hesitant to go with her because he didn't believe her son could walk again, but he knew it wasn't about him and what he thought. The mother pressed him increasingly so he went with her to the hospital. He prayed for the son but was full of incredulity when her son swung his legs over the side of the bed, stood up and walked around. He freely admitted that it wasn't anything to do with him or his limited belief that saw the boy walk again.

T.L. Osborne ministered for over thirty years in evangelising the world and his meetings were always accompanied by miraculous healings, but hear what he writes about faith: "Amongst the thousands at home and abroad who have been miraculously healed by our Lord under this ministry, only a small percentage of them have been individually prayed for. Most have been healed through their own faith, which was automatically produced in their own hearts while meditating on the Bible truths we presented from the platform or from the printed page."[97] I pray that God may use the words I have written to stir up your faith to believe God for the healing He has already promised you.

We have the incident of the disciples going across Galilee in a boat whilst Jesus slept on a cushion in the stern. When a frightening storm threatened their lives[98] the disciples woke Jesus. Jesus rebuked the storm and all was calm again. Jesus questioned them, "Where is your faith?" The purpose of including this incident in the record of the life of Jesus is not so much as to demonstrate Jesus' power over the elements, but the fact that Jesus expected the disciples to take the initiative and act on faith to quell the storm. When we face storms, we are similarly expected to take the initiative and place adverse circumstances under the power of the name of Jesus.

I once heard that the only time in eternity we will ever need to live by faith is the present. By faith we believe that Jesus

---

97  Osborne, T.L., *Miracles*, 1981, Harrison House, Oklahoma, p 23.
98  Luke 8:22-25

died and was resurrected. By faith we focus on God, and not our circumstances. By faith we receive God's promises for ourselves. Our faith has given us the power to live outside of the present and live in the heavenly realm to which Jesus has raised us.[99]

By faith we even dare to make our requests and petitions known to God.

---

99  Eph. 2:6

# Chapter 10
# The Power of Prayer for Healing

*"Ask and keep on asking and it will be given to you; seek, and keep on seeking and you will find: knock, and keep on knocking and it will be opened to you, for everyone who asks receives, and he who seeks finds, and to him who knocks, it will be opened."*
**(Matt 7:7-8** with the added sense of the Greek present tense denoting continuous action**).**

Prayer is communication and it indicates a personal relationship with God. When Jesus was super busy, when the crowds were pressing in on Him in every which way, Jesus slipped out the back door to a quiet place and spent time with His Father. Nobody, not even Jesus, can survive without communion with God. Touching the heart of God in prayer opens you up to God's values and intentions so when you are facing a problem you will need to be surrounded by prayer, both from yourself and from those around you.

Prayer is the start of the fight for your healing. The Scottish pastor and Bible teacher, Oswald Chambers, declared that: "Prayer is not a preparation for work, it IS work. Prayer is not a preparation for the battle, it IS the battle. Prayer is two-fold: definite asking and definite waiting to receive."[100]

I reached out to friends and family to pray for me to be healed of cancer and I had Christian believers, different church groups, prayer groups and a swathe of non-Christian believers from all around the world praying for me. The only proviso I requested from my non-Christian friends was that they would pray to Jesus for my healing and thank Jesus for my healing, even before it happened. I smile as I think of dozens of atheists, back-slidden Christians, Hindus, Buddhists and Muslims from everywhere praying to Jesus for my healing. With all that prayer going up to a merciful God in heaven, I felt confident of my healing.

Pete prayed with me incessantly — at every step along the way. I marvel at how quickly he sprang into warfare prayer for me at every turn and no matter what the hour. He had prayed fervently with me immediately before I was taken away to surgery, reminding me of the goodness of God, and urging me to just focus on the words of Psalm 23:4-5: "Even though I walk through the valley of the shadow of death, I will fear no evil, for You are with me; Your rod and Your staff, they comfort me. You prepare a table before me in the presence of my enemies; You anoint my head with oil; my cup runs over." He told me to focus on that banquet

---

[100] From http://kingdomservants.com/militarybattlewarconflictoffense-defensesports/ accessed 12.10.20

table in the midst of my enemies: to not think about the darkness of the valley, or any fears. He encouraged me that, even if I should die, and he hoped that wouldn't be the case, then he'd be envious because I'd be with Jesus in glory — a wonderful sure hope for those who love Jesus.

As I was being wheeled to the operating theatre past the glass panels offering beautiful views of the beaches and the ocean I felt such a calmness and stillness. Even in the midst of my enemies, facing my greatest fears, I had been given a God-provided table to feast at.

The enemy was relentless, however, for I was informed immediately before I had been given the anaesthetic that I actually had what looked suspiciously like cancerous nodes on my lungs — news that dismayed me.

It would have been so easy at that point to say I was wasting my time even having surgery when the cancer had spread so aggressively, and it took all of my mental effort to refocus on sitting down and eating at God's table. I'm glad I had that image to think upon because it gave me something to actually visualise and power to guard myself against the enemy's attacks overwhelming me. It really helped me to accept that this was God's problem — not mine.

The lumpectomy surgery went uneventfully and painlessly. I had a drainage bag attached near my armpit for the lymph fluid in my arm. With most of my underarm lymph nodes removed, that fluid was going to take time before it could be efficiently dealt with by the remaining lymph nodes.

Because my lymph drainage wasn't working well at first, I had 'cording' or Axillary Web Syndrome (AWS) — the crystallisation of the lymph fluid in my arm resulting in tightness and difficulties in stretching my arm. Pete was taught how to massage the easily-felt thick ropelike structures starting from my wrist right up to my underarm. It was most disconcerting to hear the cracking, snapping, popping and breaking of the cords under the pressure of his fingers, but I still found it difficult to stretch my arm. It wasn't until I was prayed for by Pete and another Christian man for the healing of the AWS that I was immediately able to use my arm freely again. As I waved my arm backwards and forwards and stretched it upwards I marvelled at how Jesus is always ever present to heal.

I first saw my oncologist in late May, just after my first Position Emission Tomography (PET) scan, and I had a lesson in the different types of breast cancer and treatments. (A PET can detect areas of cancer through providing images of the metabolic processes in the body's cells). The news became even worse! The results of the biopsy were at hand.

I had the aggressive HER2 positive type of breast cancer, which only accounts for about 20-25% of all breast cancers.

HER2, Human Epidermal Growth factor Receptor 2, is a protein found on the surface of healthy breast cells that causes breast cells to grow, divide and repair themselves. When the gene that controls the HER2 protein goes horribly wrong, the body creates too many of these receptors and breast cells grow and divide uncontrollably and rapidly metastasise to other parts of the body. Sometimes this is referred to as 'overexpression' of HER2.

I was informed that my surgery had been successful with clear margins, but five of the lymph nodes had had cancerous cells. Radiotherapy, hormone and endocrine therapies were ineffective against this cancer, but I was put on weekly chemotherapy together with two targeted drugs (Herceptin (trastuzumab) and Perjeta (pertuzumab)) every three weeks to enable the management of the HER2 positive cancer, but not the cure. This was made very clear to me by my oncologist.

In reading about HER2 positive breast cancer, we note: "Stage 4 breast cancer means the cancer has spread beyond the breast and local lymph nodes. At this stage, the goal of treatment is to control the growth of the cancer and prevent any organ damage or pain. Unfortunately, stage 4 breast cancer cannot be cured. But with the advent of new and innovative drugs, it's possible to stay in a period of stable disease for long periods of time."[101]

The incurability of HER2 positive cancer was confirmed by another specialist recently: "Metastatic HER2 positive breast cancer ... (is) typically not curable in the sense that we can give some type of treatment that is going to get rid of every last cell, but it is very treatable and our goals of treatment are basically to keep the cancer in the background and prolong survival and maximise quality of life so patients can get back on with their normal activities."[102] I followed the medical advice fully understanding that no one would get healed by taking that medicine, but by the same token, knowing it wouldn't stop my healing. By following that advice, I was also in a position to have regular scans, blood-tests and checks on how I was going and so be able to know definitively when I had been healed.

It was initially proposed that I would have twelve doses of chemotherapy (but I found out later that eighteen were expected). After a barrage of tests to ensure my body was up for the potent chemicals about to be pumped into it, chemo commenced early June.

---

101   https://www.healthline.com/health/breast-cancer/ask-the-expert-her2-positive#4.-What-are-the-goals-of-treatment?- accessed 7.10.20

102   Krop, Dr Ian E., "Management of HER2 Expression in Breast Cancer", www.curetoday.com, published 20.12.2019, accessed 22.2.20.

Going in to the chemo ward for the first time was scary and confronting. All about me were people with no hair, people with recurrences of cancer and women who had had single and double mastectomy surgery. It didn't look pretty and it certainly wasn't a happy place.

I used a "cold cap" to reduce the loss of hair on my scalp, but it added at least two hours to every weekly treatment. (This was essentially a tight fitting, strap on helmet that is filled with a gel that rapidly freezes the scalp once it is turned on.) I couldn't understand why not many patients opted to use the cap — in fact, I only ever saw one other person use the cap in the entire time of my treatment. The nurses told me that not many people could tolerate the coldness and actually preferred to lose their hair rather than suffer a frozen head for a couple of hours each chemo session.

Before each weekly chemo session (and the three weekly drugs to block HER2 overexpression), Pete would pray for me and the effects from the chemo and drug cocktails were very minimal.

## Chapter 11
# The Power of Words of Hope

*"Death and life are in the power of the tongue: and they that love it shall eat the fruit thereof."*
(Prov. 18:21)

You create your world by the words you use to frame it. Your words create a moral, wholesome, lovely, gracious and happy environment and you will live in a clean and honest environment, a virtuous world that God can operate in. In contrast, if you live in nastiness, hatred and backbiting you will be living in a devil controlled environment, so how could you expect God to hear your prayer for healing? You cannot be expecting a healing if you live or speak like the devil.

Paul puts it like this: "Summing it all up, friends, I'd say you'll do best by filling your minds and meditating on things true, noble, reputable, authentic, compelling, gracious — the best, not the worst; the beautiful, not the ugly; things to praise, not things to curse.

Put into practice what you learned from me, what you heard and saw and realized. Do that, and God, who makes everything work together, will work you into His most excellent harmonies."[103]

I had been a member of Pentecostal churches for a few years and knew about their beliefs for speaking positively over people and the power of prophetic words. I've personally experienced the words of prophecy. Eighteen years ago, quite out of the blue, two pastors had independently told me that I would be involved in teaching about healing in a big way.

I was a random first-time visitor to a Pentecostal church recently and I was publicly called out to be told that God had prepared ground for me and that there were wheat fields ready for harvest all around me. I was told that there appeared to be a very high tower in the midst of that field with great provision on every floor. I know that with God, even in your old age, God can breathe His Spirit into you so that, like Elizabeth, you can be fruitful for His glory. God will use you whenever and wherever He chooses as long as your focus is on Him and you walk and talk with Him in faith.

Starting the treatment for cancer was a time that I needed to be around people who actively believed for healing so in early June Pete and I decided to visit, for the first

---

[103] Phil. 4:8-9 (Message)

time, another large Pentecostal church nearby. During the last song a young man from the congregation tapped me on my shoulder and said, "I don't know who you are or anything about you, but God just spoke to me to tell you that whatever disease you are facing, God is going to completely heal you. He wants you to stand on His word and just speak the promise and not the problem." I marvel at how closely this young man was listening to the voice of God and the courage it must've taken for him to approach an absolute stranger and make that pronouncement. Those were pretty out there words to offer an older woman, yet hearing from God gives you a confidence and assurance that surpasses the vain imaginations and contortions of the human mind.

Pete was a great believer in Divine healing and had prayed for many people while he had been a pastor and had seen miracles. I grabbed books about healing from his prolific library of Christian books and started devouring them — discovering further evidence from the Bible about healing and case study after case study of amazing testimonies over many decades. Every time I went for chemo my go-to book, Bosworth's "Christ the Healer", was sitting on my tray table.

I listened continually to the podcast: "Healing Verses Read out by Reinhard Bonnke, Benny Hinn and Sid Roth" — a compendium of readings from the Bible, prayers for healing and hymns and songs about healing. Many cases of sick people merely reading or listening to scriptural verses about healing have resulted in healing. The readings were so soothing and faith assuring, that we still like to occasionally listen to the podcast while having breakfast.

Faith is stirred up when we hear the promises of God out of our own mouths. The word of God that you confess, without any fear or doubt in your heart, will be the ceiling of your faith, even to moving a mountain into the sea.[104] Jesus taught us to not talk about the mountain to God, or make a timid request about the mountain, adding "If it is your will" then boldly tell the mountain to move in the name of Jesus! How can "His will be done on earth as it is in heaven" if we don't bring God's will in heaven down to earth?

Believing confession stirs up your faith, I was saying aloud statements like: "There is no sickness in my body because I have been healed by the stripes of Jesus"; "Greater is He that is living in me than he that is in the world so devil, take your sickness away in Jesus' name"; "I am healed and delivered from the curse of the law therefore I forbid any sickness to come on my body, in the name of Jesus"; "I believe You are the Lord who heals me"; "Lord, I believe You will restore me to health and heal my disease in Jesus' name"; and "As I worship You, Lord, I believe You will take sickness away from me in Jesus' name."

---

[104] Mark 11:22-24

I have seen a woman healed of blindness. I have read her doctor's reports both before her healing and after. I talked at length with her about what happened. I know a woman who believed for Jesus healing her after she had been rendered permanently unable to walk after a car accident and she is walking around today, to the disbelief of her medical team. I was there when people were prayed for and were instantly made whole for all kinds of ailments such as broken bones, crippled legs and various heart conditions. In every case, the medical teams had said they couldn't account for the change in their health status.

A young non-Christian man who was regularly hospitalised for months on end with schizophrenia and had just been admitted for another lengthy stay in hospital was discharged the same day the spirit afflicting him had been addressed and he had been prayed for — and he has never suffered from schizophrenia again. Today he is a qualified lawyer. Interestingly, the young man wasn't even there when the spirit was commanded to leave him and was completely oblivious about what was happening in the heavenlies for him. (You may be interested to know that the young man developed schizophrenia years earlier when his non-Christian father, who had been inadvertently involved in occultic practices, had had a curse placed on him by a disgruntled witch. The curse was placed on a plant in a pot, which was placed on his father's porch in the middle of the night under a full moon.)

I saw an elderly woman prayed for to receive the Holy Spirit and, although we didn't ask for a healing, simultaneously she was miraculously healed of a severely bent back from which she'd suffered for 40 years. We saw her gradually stretch up to stand strong and tall, all the time yelling and shouting praise to Jesus.

Many years ago our Rottweiler was wracked with such pain from arthritis, whimpering and unable to move, that, after a couple of visits to the vet and learning about the hopelessness of his situation, we talked about mercifully putting him down. We had seen his x-rays and lamented at his poor state. The vet offered no remedy except ongoing medication for relief. My two youngest children overheard all of this and instantly went to the much-loved dog and prayed for him. The next thing we saw him energetically chasing after a rabbit in the paddocks and he never suffered from arthritis again.

There was an incident that John G. Lake recalled[105] of a man who came into the house where he was staying in South Africa. The man had had sunstroke, which had affected his mind, and he had gone on to develop a large cancer on his face. A little six-year-old child went over to the man and placed her hands on the cancer on his face and prayed. Within half an hour it had disappeared, but the wound

---

105  Lake, John G., *Adventures in God*, 1981, Harrison House, USA, pp 15-16.

remained for a few days after which it also disappeared. The man's mind returned to normal and he declared that the fire that had been in his brain had gone out.

God doesn't discriminate who He will heal — all He wants is a heart that believes in Him to ask in faith. That faith doesn't have to be gigantic, either, for Jesus said, "If you have faith as small as a mustard seed, you can say to this mountain, 'Move from here to there', and it will move. Nothing will be impossible for you."[106]

God doesn't have to heal according to our time schedule! Lazarus had a life-threatening illness and eventually died, but Jesus had waited two more days after He had received the plea to come and heal him before He wended His way to Bethany where Lazarus lived. Lazarus had been in his tomb for four days before Jesus raised him to life again.[107]

Jesus didn't always heal instantaneously. We have the incident of the ten lepers[108] who were healed as they went on their way to show themselves to the priests.

The healing of the blind man[109] was not an instantaneous healing but a two-stage process. Firstly, Jesus put spit

---

106  Matt. 17:20
107  John 11:1-44
108  Luke 17:11-19
109  Mark 8:23-25

onto the man's eyes and the blind man was able to see indistinctly, but after Jesus placed His hands on the blind man's eyes, then the man could see perfectly.

How many times did Peter and John go up to the temple for prayer and walk past a man who had been lame from birth and placed there to beg? Interestingly, he was placed at the temple gate, "Beautiful".[110] This Greek word, "horaios", includes the word "hora" or "hour", and it literally means "a particular hour" or "perfect in timing". The lame man was healed and in God's perfect timing, we likewise, are healed.

Jesus doesn't always heal the same illness in the same way, either. Another blind man who came to Jesus had a mud made from spit and clay smeared on his eyes and was told to go and wash in the Pool of Siloam where he regained his sight.[111]

In other words, healing from God cannot be reduced to a formula. God is always the one in control, but we can fully believe that Jesus is the same, yesterday, today and forever.[112] Peter summarised Jesus' ministry to Cornelius saying that "(Jesus) went around doing good and healing all who were under the power of the devil, because God was

---

[110] Acts 3:1-10
[111] John 9:6-7
[112] Heb. 13:8

with him."[113] If Jesus healed the sick while He was walking the earth, yesterday, then He will heal the sick today and will continue to heal the sick tomorrow.

---

[113] Acts 10:38

## Chapter 12
# The Power Over the Devil

*"Behold I give you authority to trample on serpents and scorpions, and over all the power of the enemy, and nothing shall by any means hurt you. Nevertheless do not rejoice in this, that the spirits are subject to you, but rather rejoice because your names are written in heaven."*
**(Luke 10:19-20)**

When God created Adam and Eve in the Garden of Eden, He blessed them and gave them authority over every living thing that moved on the earth. But later Satan tempted Eve to eat of the fruit that she and Adam had been forbidden to eat. She gave some to him and he also ate. In that act of rebellion Adam and Eve found themselves under a terrible curse that would include danger from animals, Eve's pain in childbirth and vulnerability in life, and hard toil that they would have to endure to produce food.

But importantly we see God's love and redemption expressed, Adam honours Eve as the mother of all living, and God provides tunics to clothe and protect them in the harsh conditions. However, they were banished from the paradise of Eden.

For the past 6,000 odd years humanity has continued to live in this fallen world, with every generation subjected to Satan's power to inflict sin, sickness, guilt, violence, shame and death. Why? In the garden, after Adam and Eve's sin had been discovered, God had spoken to Satan and given a promise for man's redemption: "And I will put enmity between you and the woman, and between your seed and her Seed: He shall bruise your head, and you shall bruise His heel."[114]

From that moment on in human history Satan has tried to stop that seed from making His promised appearance. What do you think drove Cain to kill the righteous Abel? Why do you think Sarah was barren for seventy years? Why were all the babies killed in Egypt at the time of Moses and in Bethlehem at the time of Jesus?

But the good news is that Jesus was born against the odds and He offered Himself as a sacrifice on the cross, defeated Satan and all his command. Jesus broke the grip of bondage that Satan had put all mankind under and stripped him of his power. Jesus came to destroy, loosen, dissolve and undo the works that the devil had done.[115]

---
114   Gen. 3:15
115   1 John 3:8 (Amplified Bible)

Yet the fact remains that we live in a hostile world of evil and destructive spirits attracted to decay and everything ungodly. Jesus told us clearly that "From the days of John the Baptist until now the kingdom of heaven suffers violence, and the violent take it by force."[116] Even though we can't be sure if Jesus was saying that there are hostile forces against His kingdom or if Jesus' followers violently expand His kingdom, what we can be clear on is that there is conflict, discord and warfare once we become part of Jesus' kingdom.

There is an ongoing struggle in the heavenlies to triumph over these malicious spirits and we, as the progeny of Adam and Eve, are not called to just sit in the stadium seating as spectators. The battle requires us to get down into the arena and engage with the enemy. It is only when we understand the implications of what Jesus did to Satan on the cross and we challenge Satan whenever he attacks us, that we see the afflictions and sicknesses from Satan go away.

Battle fighting principles from the secular world are equally applicable to our spiritual battle. When Julius Caesar announced: "Vine, Vidi, Vici"[117] (Latin for "I came, I saw, I conquered"), he was declaring the certainty of his

---

[116] Matt. 11:12
[117] From http://kingdomservants.com/militarybattlewarconflictoffense-defensesports/ accessed 12.10.20

belief that he would successfully vanquish his enemy. We, likewise, need to strongly declare our victory through Jesus over our enemy in the skirmishes that beset us. The war has already been won through Jesus at the cross and our enemy has been rendered powerless at the cross. We need to confidently assert that belief when he attacks us in order for Satan to capitulate — until the next time.

I thank God that He had blessed me with seeing that demon in my bedroom, hissing vehemently at me just after I had been filled with the Holy Spirit. Even though I didn't believe in the existence of a supernatural devil at the time, the viciousness of that encounter has long stayed with me to remind me that we really are in a battle for our lives against the most evil, deceptive, devious and hostile of opponents. Whilst Jesus crushed the head of Satan at Calvary, the application of that victory over the powers of evil is in the hands of Christians on a daily basis. Satan is very much alive and well in the world today trying to rob mankind of the full effect of Christ's finished work on the cross.

Pete, my husband, had a similar encounter just after he had been saved. A respectable, smartly dressed gentleman suddenly appeared before him and Pete asked the man what his name was. The man replied, "Lucifer." Pete had been warned about Satan so he said, "I know who you are, Satan. Go away!" Satan replied that he would show Pete just how powerful he was and placed his hand on Pete's forehead and started to draw on his brain. Pete valiantly resisted until he realised that things were way out of his control and that his brain was being squeezed like toothpaste from a tube through his skull. He courageously tried to stammer out, "In the name of Jesus ..." which he'd been taught to use if Satan attacked him, but he couldn't get the phrase out no matter how hard he tried. After a long struggle Pete finally managed to blurt out "Jesus!" and he felt intense burning behind his ears and a fierce wind blowing Satan away. He saw Satan topping and tailing like a tumbling leaf as he receded into the distance.

Frequently people get involved in what I term the "devil's toys" — activities and objects like mind reading, séances, water divining, ESP, witchcraft, crystals, psychic healing, tarot cards, UFOs, angel guides and fortune telling. You can't play around with this sort of thing without penalty. If you are in agreement with Satan, and that's what is happening if you are mixing with wonders from his world, then Satan has the licence to destroy you or your family.

Throughout our lives totally surrendered to Jesus, we overcome the devil by the blood of the Lamb (our inward faith) and by the word of our testimony (our outward faith).[118] It is our faith in action that overcomes all the

---

118  Rev. 12:11

afflictions of Satan — his attacks that invariably fall on our relationships, our finances and our health. Let me demonstrate.

My husband had been an itinerant hippy travelling the world before he had been marvellously and miraculously saved in Perth. A short time later he had been beset by a horde of demons plucking at him, sneering and mocking him. Although he kept commanding them to go in the name of Jesus, they just looked menacingly at him before they eventually dilatorily left. When he recounted this to his pastor, he was asked if he had any relics of idolatry in his possession. Indeed he had. He had a combi-van full of rice paper Tibetan artwork of demons, yin and yang drawings and Buddhist relics. He unhesitatingly promptly smashed and burnt them and he has never been bothered by demons physically attacking him again.

I am recounting these events to illustrate that Christians really are in a battle against evil forces. We need to practise definite resistance and like Jesus, command: "Get thee behind me, Satan."[119] We must use the promises of Scripture as weapons against the "strong man". Jesus has given all His disciples the know-how, when and why coupled with the power of the Holy Spirit to defeat satanic forces.[120] We need

---

119   Matt. 16:23
120   Luke 24:49 and Acts 2:38-39.

to stop being doves and become the Lord's eagles using the arsenals of warfare that Jesus has given us.

Jesus won the war for us through His death, he saved us, and we have the Helper that he sent us to triumphantly fight the battle against the devil. "Thanks be to God, who gives us the victory through our Lord Jesus Christ."[121]

Too many people in the world blindly follow this evil opponent, foolishly perceiving him as an "angel of light"[122] and his attractions as wonderful revelations. When I was working in Iran I was amazed at what looked like an entire country having given itself over to witchcraft and the occult. I was frequently invited to tea leaf readings, palm readings and tarot card readings and whenever we went to a public park there was inevitably a man walking around with a trained Australian budgerigar. If you paid the man some money, the budgerigar would select a card that would supposedly predict your future. (I felt indignant that one of our beautiful native birds should be captured and trained for such nefarious purposes!)

What really shocked me, though, in Iran were the three or more strands of unravelled cassette tape that had been carefully and purposefully strewn along the highway through the desert from Tehran to Abyaneh, a distance

---

[121] 1 Cor. 15:57
[122] 2 Cor. 11:14

of about 320 kilometres. These tapes used to be found carefully strewn around intersections in Sydney and were found to have the recorded voices of Satanists or witches cursing Jesus, His followers and families, bringing destruction to the lives of so many. It seems highly plausible, therefore, that some evil people had carefully positioned these tapes along the roads so that those driving past would come under those spoken curses. (I don't want to dwell on the power of spells and curses here, but will just say that they are mentioned around 200 times in the Bible, they carry satanic power, were strictly forbidden in the Old Testament[123] and that Christians can need deliverance from curses.[124])

We don't have to leave the Western world, though, to see Satanism, sorcery, witchcraft and black magic being practised. Sure there are organised movements like satanic churches, Wiccas and Masonic Lodges, but there are many other forms of demonic evil in our society that are accepted quite freely, like kinesiology, the Holistic Health Movement, the "healing power of the universe", cosmic energy, crystals and New Age practices. It used to be a common practice for teenagers to be involved in séances and ouija boards and still far too many people seek out a fortune teller to

---

[123] Deut. 18:10-12
[124] For further reading, see *Evicting Demonic Intruders* by Noel and Phyl Gibson (1993, Freedom In Christ Ministries, Australia).

reveal their future. Many of our international visitors have recounted to me mind-boggling incidents of powerful encounters with Satan while in Australia.

Disgruntled gypsies, witches and Satanists sometimes curse families resulting in a generational curse. I'm sure you can think of families where there has been a strange repetition of a particular curse generation after generation. People within a family may die from accidental causes generation after generation and the media will unwittingly refer to these incidents as the Such and Such Family Curse.

There are people with psychic powers that may be a gift of discernment from God, but they can also be a counterfeit from the evil realm. The demon-possessed can sense things about people, have the ability to foretell the future and have an insight into people without having any knowledge of them. I knew of a woman who saw in a dream the attack on the twin towers two weeks before it happened. Another time she told her neighbour to get her house number painted clearly because her husband's life would be on the line and the ambulance would need to be able to quickly identify her house. A week later, with the delay from the ambulance struggling to identify her house, the husband died of a heart attack. She told a friend that she was pregnant before the friend knew.

I was walking under a railway tunnel in the city looking at

the cuff of my blouse where a friend's breast-fed baby had earlier posseted and was simultaneously pondering about a lady about to have a breast lump removed and her ability to breast feed afterwards. Sitting in the tunnel was a strange looking young man with peculiar eyes. He started to drone aloud to me, over and over again as I passed, "Some people can breast feed and some people can't." How was that even possible without an evil spirit informing him of my thoughts?

I know of another lady who can hold any object belonging to a person and can accurately diagnose their sickness, right down to the medical terminology, even though she has no medical background. That lady can also have objects levitate at will. Such powers are not of God.

Divination, magic, psychic powers, and necromancy were rightly condemned in the Bible. We have the incident of Paul and Silas delivering the slave girl who had a spirit of divination on her to show us how Jesus wants us to deal with people who are enslaved to evil spirits.[125]

The devil has assembled his invisible army and gained access to our culture like a Trojan horse. The Bible has been abundantly clear about his tactics calling him the arch deceiver, adversary, "accuser of the brethren", a "roaring

---

125 Acts 16:16-19

lion looking for someone to devour", the " father of lies" and a "murderer from the beginning". Any association with the demonic realm, be it innocently dabbling to being actively involved; be it having sex with demon-affected people and having their demons come to live in you; or being led by the devil into crime; or from generations earlier in your history being involved in the occult, there will always be a price to pay. Satan is a hard paymaster.

You don't get to play in Satan's toy-box or live a devil-inspired life without a huge cost to yourself. Alcoholism, drug addiction, prostitution, insanity, financial disaster, accidents, sickness and even death are all fruits of playing around in the devil's realm.

One woman I knew had witch powers and visited witches in the middle of the night, but her husband was killed in a car crash and her children regularly had near-fatal accidents. Another person I knew who boasted about his astral travels into people's houses was tormented with depression, suicide and homosexuality. A person I knew who was hospitalised with a psychotic episode was asked, very early on in the medical interview, if they had ever been involved with witchcraft. One man I knew, who had actively engaged in paranormal phenomena, became effectively a compulsive gambler in multimillion dollar deals that never eventuated. He possessed what the Japanese refer to as a "Binbogami", a spirit being that brings poverty.

Anyone who lives in cultures where there is open worship of idols see demonic activity more readily and are on their guard against demonic influence. Australians are well familiar with aboriginal bone pointing and the inevitable death that follows, even despite medical attention. Spirit houses are placed in front of so many homes in Asia and every day offerings are given to appease the spirits and ensure their beneficence towards the occupants of the house. I have an Asian friend who has placed mirrors on a wall of her house to ward off evil spirits afflicting her household from a hostile neighbour.

Jesus warned us that demons are ever ready to afflict a person when he related that when a person has been delivered of a demon, if he isn't guarded by the Holy Spirit then that demon would return with even more loathsome demons to live in that man, leaving him far worse off.[126] The warning is very much for us today. If we haven't let the Holy Spirit come into our lives to fill every part of us, or have allowed hurt or resentment get a foothold in our lives, then an evil spirit or evil spirits can accompany that resentment and control us. The hedge of protection from God will have gone. On the contrary, if we resist the devil he will flee from us.[127]

When we become Christians, if we don't deal with these

---
[126] Luke 11: 24-26
[127] James 4:7

leftovers from our old way of life like ungodly anger, unforgiveness, jealousy, fear, greed, resentment, they will reappear in our lives. As we go through life, situations arise and the old nature can resurface. If we don't deal with the emotional pain and ask God to heal us through His Holy Spirit and to forgive any person who wronged us, then the emotional pain can take hold of us and an opportunistic evil spirit may accompany that wound. Too many people are living with psychological issues in this day and age when all they need to do is to look to Jesus for their healing just as He healed the woman with the physical 'issue of blood'.

History is littered with people who had issues that grew out of resentment or fear. Hitler was harshly abused by his father and he transferred his hatred of his father to the Jews, with disastrous results. Martin Bryant believed that a property his father tried to purchase was sold to somebody else unfairly and his anger simmered until he killed 35 people at Port Arthur in revenge. More recently, the Claremont serial killer killed in direct retaliation for setbacks in his own relationships.

From the beginning of the Bible to the very end, we are made aware of Satan's presence. Eve was tempted by Satan; Satan was there at Job's affliction; some Satanic force opposed an angel answering Daniel's prayer until Michael the archangel came to assist him; Satan challenged Jesus when he commenced His ministry and went into the desert; Paul talked about a 'messenger of Satan' afflicting him and in Revelation we have the great war of Satan against the Christians.

Jesus spent the majority of His ministry dealing with widespread demon possession, demonic oppression and affliction. Evil spirits fled at the word of Jesus because they knew He was God and had ultimate power.

In the New Testament demons and sickness are linked,[128] where they cast out many demons and anointed with oil many that were sick and where Jesus gave His twelve disciples power and authority over all devils and to cure diseases.[129] In Acts 10:38: "God anointed Jesus of Nazareth with the Holy Spirit and with power, who went about doing good and healing all who were oppressed by the devil, for God was with Him." In Luke 4:40-41 we read that, "When the sun was setting, all those who had any that were sick with various diseases brought them to Him; and He laid His hands on every one of them, and healed them. And demons also came out of many, crying out, and saying, 'You are the Christ, the Son of God!' And He, rebuking them, did not allow them to speak, for they knew that He was the Christ." Matthew says of that same incident that "When evening had come, they brought to Him many who

---

[128] e.g. Mark 6:13
[129] Luke 9:1-2

were demon-possessed. And He cast out the spirits with a word, and healed all who were sick."[130]

For our purposes of understanding Satan and the sicknesses that he inflicts on people, let's look at a sample of the sicknesses that are recorded as being directly from his hand. The Bible has attributed to demonic influence supernatural strength and insanity of the man living amongst the tombs;[131] self-destructive tendencies with the young boy thrown into the fire;[132] dumbness;[133] blindness and dumbness;[134] inexplicable intelligence, a spirit of divination;[135] and a bent spine.[136] Invariably a spirit's main activities are to torture, maim and to drive to compulsion.

God is not the author of sickness. The people Jesus healed were not made sick by God. Rather, Jesus distinctly attributed sickness to the devil when He said things like the woman being bound eighteen years by Satan.[138] Jesus went about doing His Father's will and to do that He destroyed the works of the devil. Hebrews 2:14 makes it very clear that, "Inasmuch then as the children have partaken of flesh and blood, He Himself likewise shared in the same, that

---

130  Matt. 8:16
131  Mark 5:4, 15-16
132  Mark 9:22
133  Matt. 9:32-33
134  Matt. 12:22
135  Acts 16:16
136  Luke 13:16

through death He might destroy him who had the power of death, that is, the devil."

Just to be clear, not all sicknesses mean the direct presence of an unclean spirit, but all bondage to sickness comes from Satan. The only way you can know for sure what is the root cause of a sickness is through the discernment of the indwelling Holy Spirit. On this score I know of Christian people who see shadows around people who are afflicted, or shadows over the part of the body affected by demons and others who actually see the demon on the person. I haven't actually seen a demon afflicting a person, but I have "known" that a person was afflicted. I saw a new person come forward to become a Christian, recently, and I knew that she had an evil spirit. Sure enough, when she was prayed for we had a full on manifestation, thrashing and shrieking and screaming until she was delivered of the demon.

I have been in the shopping centre and felt incredible evil on two elderly people ahead of me in a queue. Another time, at a dinner party I sensed that there was an endless dark chasm behind me and I was hurtling down it at a frightening speed. It was so terrifying that I gasped aloud and turned around and saw the host standing behind me. Six months later our host's photo was plastered all over the newspapers as the head of a ruthless and murderous crime gang.

If evil spirits were around in Jesus' day causing illnesses, then they are around in this day and age afflicting all kinds of people. I believe sickness is a lie of Satan. I know Christians get sick, but that sickness does not have to remain in the Christian's body if the Christian uses the power gifted him by Jesus to fight it. The Christian, the child of God who has committed body, soul and spirit to God, shouldn't need healing of anything and should see any sickness, be it a headache, depression, cancer, multiple sclerosis or addiction, as an attack from Satan that can't take a hold of them because Jesus has freed Christians from the bonds of Satan and given us the weapons against him.

Quite clearly, salvation isn't limited to the forgiveness of sins but also includes freedom from the effects of sin: disease and death. The healing is within and the healing is without. Whoever has faith to believe in Jesus for deliverance can be set free in mind, body and spirit. Since the message of the cross is the power of God,[137] then whoever believes in the gospel of Christ has accessed "the power of God to salvation for everyone who believes, for the Jew first and also for the Greek."[138] Again, the word 'salvation' here is from that same root word as found in the name of Jesus and we go back to the earlier conclusion that power has been given to us for forgiveness and for healing.

---

[137] I Cor. 1:18
[138] Rom. 1:16

No wonder Jesus taught His disciples to pray: "And do not lead us into temptation, but deliver us from the evil one, For Yours is the kingdom and the power and the glory forever."[139]

---

[139] Matt. 6:13

## Chapter 13
## The Power of the Name

*"And these signs will follow those who believe:
in My name they will cast out demons; they
will speak with new tongues; they will take up
serpents; and if they drink anything deadly, it will
by no means hurt them; they will lay hands on the
sick, and they will recover."*
**(Mark 16:17-18)**

The name you have been given has a meaning, but most parents give their children names without really looking at the meaning of that name. Once I was playing a game with our children about the meanings of their names. It became almost a competition about who had the best meaning for their name, but it was a lay down misère for the one whose name meant "the winner".

Spurred on by the competitive interest amongst her siblings our youngest piped up and asked what her name meant and since I had no idea I checked. There was a look of dismay on her face when we all read that the diminutive form of her name, by which she was known, meant "tree bark". It took a bit of deft footwork to show that her full name really meant "Beautiful princess" — a name she felt quite suitably described her.

In Bible times a name often indicated the purpose or mission of a person or of some impending event. Isaiah, for example, was asked by God to give his son a short story for a name: "Maher-shalal-hash-baz" (which prophesied the looming raid of Samaria and Damascus by Assyria). Abram had his name changed by God to "Abraham", which had a change in meaning from 'father' to 'father of many'.

Jesus, after he had humbled Himself for the redemption of mankind, was given "The name which is above every name, that at the name of Jesus every knee should bow, of those in heaven, and of those on earth, and of those under the earth, and that every tongue should confess that Jesus Christ is Lord, to the glory of God the Father."[140] Can you see the power and authority that has been given to the name of Jesus?

That power vested in His name has been given to those who profess the name of Jesus. The Christian has power in the name of Jesus to command evil spirits to leave and to lay hands on the sick so that they recover. Furthermore, Jesus told His disciples that "Whatever you ask in My name, that I will do, that the Father may be glorified in the Son. If ye

---

[140] Phil. 2:9-11

ask anything in My name, I will do it."[141] Jesus expects the word dwelling in us by the Holy Spirit to have the same healing power today when we call on His name.

The committed Christian can expect to be living in continuous health because he is filled with the life of God. Christians are not immune to sickness and disease that come through the work of Satan in this fallen world, but they do have the authority to command that sickness or disease to leave through the healing power encompassed in the name of Jesus. Too many Christians are complacent about God's heart for them and the grace He extends through the indwelling of the Holy Spirit and what they can claim as God's children and they ignorantly allow themselves to continue in suffering as being God's will for them, or God's testing of their character.

I had to learn that there are times when God doesn't answer prayer as we would wish. Nearly 20 years ago my friend's father, in his sixties, had died suddenly from a heart attack. Being the new and enthusiastic Christians that we were, we marched into the funeral parlour and prayed for him to be resurrected. Nothing happened. We were confused and disappointed. It was many months later that God spoke to me about the matter. He explained that in every case of resurrection in the Bible, the person had died prematurely.

---

[141] John 14:13-14

Then God explained that my friend's father had lived his life and that He had taken him. I learnt the hard way that God is God!

I have been stating that the committed Christian has authority over Satan and his destructive demons because anyone who isn't a committed Christian and thinks that merely stating "in the name of Jesus" will give them authority is badly mistaken. The seven sons of Sceva[142] are a case in point. They ended up being completely discomfited by a possessed madman when they tried to use the name "Jesus" without any knowledge of who He was.

One of the people who was asked to leave the cult (as a result of refusing to cease contact with other Christians and me) became excited at the power he had over the devil after he was spirit-filled. (Remember that in the group we hadn't even known there was such a thing as a supernatural devil.) He and his mate were praying for a giant of a man who was new to Christianity when suddenly the man started frothing and growling. The demon inside the man started shouting that they didn't have the authority to order him to depart. The man was flinging his body about wildly like in an epileptic fit. For new Christians, they were right out of their depth. They stood their ground in the name of Jesus and quoted scriptures at the demon, all the while declaring

---

[142] Acts 19:13-17

that they had the authority to cast him out because they were children of the living God. After an hour the demon finally left and the man was calm. Strangely, the man couldn't recall what had happened.

Just as a clarification — demons will flee immediately when you speak over them in the name of Jesus, but if there is any area that allows the devil to have a toehold in your life, demons won't respect you. I believe this is why my friend, as a new Christian, didn't have full power over the enemy because he still hadn't cleaned up his life and Satan had a claim on him.

We really are in a battle fighting evil forces. Through the power of the Holy Spirit we can defeat these evil spirits, we can strip them of their authority in our bodies by the power in the name of Jesus. Jesus won the war for us against Satan, but we will continue to fight the battle until the day we go on to glory. Peter told the Christians to "Be sober, be vigilant; because your adversary the devil walks about like a roaring lion, seeking whom he may devour. Resist him, steadfast in the faith, knowing that the same sufferings are experienced by your brotherhood in the world."[143]

Sickness is not there to test your character. It is not about waiting for healing — today is the day of salvation.[144] If we

---
143  1 Pet. 5:8-9
144  Luke 19:9

can be prayed for today to be saved from our sins, we can be delivered from our sicknesses today, also. The two-fold work of salvation by Jesus, the healing of spirit and physical healing of mind and soul, happens as soon as we pray. That salvation and healing are there for everybody who calls on the name of the Lord. Once you grasp that the name of Jesus means to be made whole spiritually and physically, you can be free of your sickness.

Order the spirit of infirmity/cancer/depression or whatever disease you are facing to leave you in Jesus' name and then meekly pray: "I am healed because of what Jesus has done and I receive my healing now!" and "Let it happen then, just as I believe."[145]

---

[145] Matt. 9:29

## Chapter 14

# The Power of Your Praise

*"I will praise Your name, O LORD, for it is good. For He has delivered me out of all trouble."*
**(Psalm 54:6-7)**

Have you ever been in a situation that looked absolutely hopeless? Have you ever had one thing after another happening and there didn't look like there was any way to get out of it? I wonder if you've ever felt like Paul and Silas did? They were in a city where nobody knew them. They were unfairly accused and set upon by a crowd of people yelling, grabbing, pulling and shoving at them.

And then there was that beating. They were stripped naked and flogged severely with a hard length of wood. We aren't told how many times they were hit, but many men have died from these fierce beatings.

They were thrown into an airless, dank and dark prison cell. They had their arms and legs placed in stocks so that they couldn't move. Can you imagine the excruciating agony and pain they must have been in?

So what would you have done? Moaned and groaned? Wept aloud? Yelled invectives at the top of your lungs? How would you have made it to the next day? How would you have even made it to the other side of midnight? I don't think anyone could have slept.

I had a glimpse of the trauma they must have experienced when I was once in a car in crowded downtown Jericho when a mob of people ran towards us and started to hammer on the car and wave their fists belligerently. (Note to self — avoid being in Arab territory in a car with Israeli numberplates when there are marked hostilities between Arabs and Israelis.) That little incident alone made me sleepless for a few nights, but Paul and Silas were going through far worse.

Paul and Silas did the only thing they could do. Their spirit was the only thing that the brutal Roman penal system couldn't touch, so they sang their hearts out in praise to God Almighty (El Shaddai). They called on the power that they had available, and God came and shook that prison with an earthquake so powerful, so strong, that the prison doors fell open, their stocks were unloosed and the gaoler woke up, alarmed.

The earthquake shook an area in Philippi, but there was a power that shakes not only the earth, the sea and the dry land, but also the heavens.[146] What happened next was the full demonstration of that power of God for humankind — the gaoler knelt before the two men and asked them what he had to do to be saved.

There is only one answer. There is only one Saviour. There is only one Redeemer of humankind. They answered the gaoler with the only answer available for all people that will bring us into a relationship with the all-powerful sustainer and nourisher of life — believe in the Lord Jesus, and then you and your household will be saved.

When our praises are singularly directed to the Lord Jesus Christ as our Saviour and Redeemer of humankind, we have found the secret to the power of the forgiveness of sins and also the secret to the power for the healing of all diseases. The power of your praise weaves those two concepts together throughout the entire Bible. God rescues us from the enemy of sin and its effects when we extol and revere our Saviour God.

When we embrace Jesus as our Lord and Saviour we embark on an extraordinary life of discovery and adventure where our arms are made to be strong; we are helped and we are blessed with the blessings of heaven above and of deep waters that lie beneath the ground.[147] In other

---
146 Heb. 12:26; Hag. 2:6.
147 Gen 49:24, 25 adapted

words, in Christ we will live an abundantly fruitful and powerful life.

You are not your past. You are who God says you are. Your identity is not defined by what is happening to you in your present circumstances, nor what happened to you in the past, but what will happen to you in your future.

I like Revelation 1:5-6 where it says (Jesus) "Loved us, and washed us from our sins in His own blood, and has made us kings and priests to His God and Father."[148] What is actually being said here is that Jesus freed us once and for all but loves us always. That love is as present for us in this moment as it was at the time when Jesus was overwhelmed by the dreadfulness of the cross. Think how much love Jesus has for us that He died in such a publicly humiliating way that we could be washed from our sins.

God's love for you is in the present moment. We saw the great force of God's love demonstrated when He gave His only begotten Son over to degradation and death for us, but that wasn't the end of God's great love. Jesus' love for us is incomprehensible and unending.

---

148 The tenses in the Greek are specifically selected to show the author's perspective on the action. In this case, "loved" is the dative of the articular present active participle of "agapao", but there is a change of tense for "washed" (or loosed, released, dissolved, destroyed, set at naught, annulled). In this instance it is the first aorist active participle of "luo".

Our sins were forgiven in the past. We don't have to wait for some future absolution after waiting and working towards forgiveness. Forgiveness was declared when Jesus left the tomb, and all we have to do to be forgiven is believe it. John 3:16-17 says: "For God so loved the world that He gave His only begotten Son, that whoever believes in Him should not perish but have everlasting life. For God did not send His Son into the world to condemn the world, but that the world through Him might be saved."

It seems that we are overwhelmed with blessings when we know that we are endlessly loved by God and that He has made us perfect through the cost of His own lifeblood — but there is more. God has promised that today we are anointed as princes and priests and our destiny will be for immortal regencies and eternal priesthoods. Every single believer today reigns alongside Jesus and wields a power so mighty that the hordes of hell cannot resist.

Our praises then spontaneously fall from our lips to praise our God. "Every creature which is in heaven, and on the earth and under the earth and such as are in the sea, and all that are in them, I heard saying, 'Blessing, and honour and glory and power be to Him who sits on the throne, and to the Lamb, forever and ever!'"[149]

---

[149] Rev 5:13

So what do our praises unleash? In many of the Psalms we find David afflicted or desperate and needy. Inevitably he is struggling until he turns around and praises God. David has found the key to God acting on his behalf — praise.

Take Psalm 142 for example. In verse 2 he is pouring out his complaint to God and telling him all his troubles. In verse 3 his spirit is completely overwhelmed and he is paranoid that his enemies have set a snare for him. In verse 4 he is abandoned by his friends and alone. In verse 6 he says he is very despondent. It can't get any worse for David so what is the remedy? What he does is a complete turnaround from self-pity to praise when he fights back with verse 7, a request that his soul be brought out of prison so that he can praise God and God can bless him. In that one verse we see David confessing his position, praising God and having faith that God will uphold His promises towards David. David has given us the template for having the power of God working not only in his life, but in our lives as well.

For further confirmation of the power of praise we have a glimpse of its power in the protection of a nation. The false prophet, Balaam, found he couldn't place a curse on Israel, much to the chagrin of the wicked prince, Balak. Balaam explained to Balak that it was impossible to place a curse on Israel because "The LORD his God is with him, and the shout of a King is among them."[150] Because the people were joyfully acclaiming the presence of God, their triumphant king, who brought them out of Egypt, they were rendered as strong and formidable as a wild bull,[151] and Balaam was unable to bring evil upon them through a curse.

So many people are healed of sicknesses as they are worshipping and praising God. Singing and dancing before God in praise and worship creates an atmosphere where God's power can be manifested. Since God inhabits the praises of His people[152] He is living among us when we praise Him and all sickness must flee in His presence.

In praising God, we are declaring His sovereignty over all of our life and declaring that the devil is not lord over us. Remember the record of the king of Judah, Jehoshaphat, going out to battle against the armies of the Moabites and Ammonites?[153] He was told by a prophet not to be worried, but to just go out and watch what God was going to do. Jehoshaphat sent out the temple singers ahead of the army of Judah, singing and praising God with "loud and high voices" for His everlasting goodness. As a result of the spiritual warfare that Judah was mustering, the marauding armies were ambushed and routed — a total victory.

---

[150] Num. 23:21
[151] Num. 23:22
[152] Psa. 22:3
[153] 2 Chr. 20

I'd like to share one incident that happened in my life to illustrate how God is present when we praise Him. I was with some of our ex-cult members for an impromptu song and praise night in our local church building, which happened to be a windowless factory unit. There were about twelve of us and it was a Sydney autumn so the doors were shut and the air-conditioning was not turned on. As we were singing, we each in turn started to have our faces brushed and stroked with a delightful and gentle breeze. In the Hebrew and the Greek the word for "spirit" can mean "wind" or "breath", and here we were being privileged to have the breath of God touching us individually. We had an older retired pastor leading the singing that evening and he was overwhelmed with emotion when he told us that in all his life of walking with God, he had never experienced anything like this. What a precious time it was!

So we need to be anxious about nothing and in all our troubles, once we have approached our God in prayer, we can then offer our thanksgiving and praise and wait to see His healing power.

"Be anxious for nothing, but in everything by prayer and supplication, with thanksgiving, let your requests be made known to God."[154]

---

154  Phil. 4:6

# Chapter 15
# The Power of Communion

*"Imitate me, just as I also imitate Christ. Now I praise you, brethren, that you remember me in all things and keep the traditions just as I delivered them on to you ...*

*For I received from the Lord that which I also delivered to you: that the Lord Jesus on the night in which He was betrayed took bread; and when He had given thanks, He broke it and said, 'Take, eat; this is My body which is broken for you; do this in remembrance of Me.'*

*In the same manner, he also took the cup after supper, saying, 'This cup is the new covenant in My blood. This do, as often as you drink it, in remembrance of Me.' For as often as you eat this bread and drink this cup, you proclaim the Lord's death till He comes.*

> *Therefore whoever eats the bread or drinks this cup of the Lord in an unworthy manner will be guilty of the body and blood of the Lord. But let a man examine himself, and so let him eat of the bread and drink of the cup.*
>
> *For he who eats and drinks in an unworthy manner eats and drinks judgment on himself, not discerning the Lord's body. For this reason many are weak and sick among you, and many sleep. For if we would judge ourselves, we would not be judged. But when we are judged, we are chastened of the Lord, that we may not be condemned with the world."*
>
> (1 Corinthians 11:1-2, 23-32)

From late May I commenced having regular morning teas with a dear Christian sister. At these morning teas she would pray for me, offer me biblical encouragement for healing and then have communion with me. She related to me that so many people had been healed while having communion and that the preacher, Joseph Prince, at one point in his life, had daily communion with his wife, understanding that there was power in eating the bread and drinking the wine for bringing life and health. Smith Wigglesworth, the healing evangelist, took communion daily, often on his own, to counteract any pride within himself. By remembering that "As often as you eat this bread and drink this cup, you proclaim the Lord's death till He comes,"[155] he was keeping his eyes on Calvary and not on himself.

How many people take the bread and wine and never realise its incredible importance and implications for them? Some people take communion as a tradition, others as a habit and others as a ritual to confirm their belonging to a group, but taking communion is so serious a matter that it can bring blessing or judgment.

Communion or the fellowship meal or the Lord's Supper is a meal of bread and wine, instituted by Jesus, to remind us of the twofold purpose of Jesus' ministry — the forgiveness of sins through the blood, represented by the wine, and the healing of our souls and bodies represented by the bread. Jesus' very name, "God saves", embodies this complete divine healing — spiritual healing: the sinner being saved from his sins and declared righteous and physical healing of physical and mental diseases through the stripes and bruising of Jesus. Communion is all about being made physically and mentally whole.

Jesus in the Greek is Ἰησοῦς, or Iésous. The "sous" part of the word is from the base word, "sozo". When I had searched

---

[155] 1 Cor. 11:26

through the New Testament and coloured in the over 100 times where the word "sozo" or one of its derivatives had been used, I found that 38 times it has been translated "save" and referred to forgiving people of their sins.[156]

Another 53 times it was used in the past tense, "saved" with reference to the forgiveness of sins, but at the other times when it was used, it was translated as "healed".[157]

We referred to the "Power of your Faith" in Chapter 9, but please note that the healing was frequently linked with the faith of the individual. When the woman with an issue of blood fought her way through the crowd to touch the hem of Jesus' clothes, she said to herself, 'If only I may touch His clothes, I shall be made well.'"[158] Matthew says of this incident that Jesus said to her, "'Be of good cheer, daughter; your faith has made you well.' And the woman was healed at that moment."[159] Paul looked intently at a crippled man and saw that he had faith to be healed[160] and Jesus told the leper to "Rise and go; your faith has made you well."[161]

---

156 Matt. 1:21: "She will bring forth a Son, and you shall call His name JESUS, for He will save His people from their sins."
157 Mark 5:23: "He pleaded earnestly with Him, 'My little daughter is dying. Please come and put your hands on her so that she will be healed and live.'"
158 Mark 5:28
159 Matt. 9:22
160 Acts 14:9
161 Luke 17:19

The use of the word "sozo", however, goes one step further than referring to healing from sins and healing from diseases. It has also been used to refer to healing from evil spirits. There was an incident where a demoniac had terrorised the region of the Gadarenes near Galilee and he had fled his chains to live a solitary existence, bereft of clothes, amongst the tombs. Jesus had ordered the evil spirits in him to go into a herd of pigs and these had rushed down the hillside and drowned in the lake. Luke records that "Those who had seen it told them by what means he who had been demon-possessed was healed."[162]

A demon or evil spirit aims to torture, enslave and drive a person to some sort of compulsion or addiction — to "steal, and to kill, and to destroy."[163] Demons fight against you living in peace. They ruin relationships, finances and health. Their sole aim is to see the unsaved permanently tortured after death.

When demonic power is the cause of a person's illness, generally no amount of modern medicine is going to get them well. There are recorded cases where aborigines have pointed a bone, "kurdaitcha", at someone and despite medical intervention, the person died from inexplicable causes. We are told about Jesus healing a woman at the synagogue with a rigidly fused spine. She is said to have

---

[162] Luke 8:36
[163] John 10:10

been bound by Satan for over 18 years. Even if modern day medicines cannot cure that condition, when the Christian demands the evil spirit leave in the name of Jesus, we can expect instant healing.

To summarise, the communion meal remembers Jesus saving us from our sins, healing us from our diseases and delivering us from the enemy, Satan.

We've read that the bread represents the body of Jesus and if you understand this, and eat the bread reverently, fittingly, with due consideration, you won't be weak and sick. If you discern what Jesus' body did, and what the bread represents, if you understand that Jesus took all your diseases onto His body so that you could be free of disease, then you will walk in health and be free from disease. If you don't, then you will get sick and may even die.

But let's explore further about what the body of Jesus is all about. The principle of the bread representing our healing is reiterated time and time again in the Bible. Just how powerful it is is illustrated in the incident where a Gentile woman came to Jesus for the healing of her daughter.

A Canaanite woman from that vicinity came to him, crying out, "'Have mercy on me, O Lord, Son of David! My daughter is severely demon-possessed.' He [Jesus] answered her not a word. And His disciples came and urged Him saying, 'Send her away, for she cries out after us.' But He answered and said, 'I was not sent except to the lost sheep of the house of Israel.' Then she came and worshipped Him, saying, 'Lord, help me!' But He answered and said, 'It is not good to take the children's bread and throw it to the little dogs.' And she said, 'Yes Lord, yet even the little dogs eat the crumbs which fall from their masters' table.' Then Jesus answered and said to her, 'O woman, great is your faith! Let it be to you as you desire.' And her daughter was healed from that very hour."[164]

The woman had been insistent and acknowledged that the bread (representing healing) belonged to the children of Israel, but, as a Gentile, she could expect to receive only the leftovers. She begged for merely the crumbs of the bread that Jesus offered so that her daughter could be healed. A fragment from the beaten and scourged body of Jesus is sufficient to heal. In so many incidents in the life of Jesus, it was the Gentiles who grasped the import of His ministry long before the Jews did. No wonder Jesus remarked that she had great faith and her request was granted.

Communion is a meal instituted by Jesus during the Last Supper and observed in Christian congregations on a regular basis throughout the world. Jesus gave His disciples bread and wine to remember Him. What the bread and

---

[164] Matt. 15:22-28

wine represent was prophesied in Isaiah 53:3. We are left with little doubt about what Jesus accomplished and what the doctrine of the Atonement is all about — God's promise through Jesus to forgive our sins and heal our diseases: "He was bruised for our iniquities; the chastisement for our peace was upon Him, and by His stripes we are healed."[165]

It was Matthew who took this very verse to apply it in the context of Jesus healing. We read of Jesus coming down the mountainside and going into Capernaum. On the way He healed a leper, the centurion's paralysed servant, Peter's feverish mother-in-law and here He was, as the sun was setting, with crowds of sick and demon-possessed people gathering outside Peter's house. We then read: "When evening had come, they brought to Him many who were demon-possessed. And He cast out the spirits with a word, and healed all who were sick, that it might be fulfilled which was spoken by Isaiah the prophet, saying: 'He Himself took our infirmities and bore our sicknesses.'"[166]

Of all the scenes in the Bible, I think this one stands out for its beauty and the generosity of God's gift to mankind. I love visualising that scene in Capernaum. I can see the red sky and reflections in a calm Galilee. The air would be still. Everyone had finished their work for the day and were making their way over the hard stony ground to

---
165  Isa. 53:5
166  Matt 8:16-17

Peter's house to meet with the man who promised them health and life. The tiny house would have been lit with oil filled lamps and everyone was expectant. No-one returned home disappointed. All the sick were healed and delivered of demons.

God demonstrates that He has forgiven sins by healing an individual. This is why it says in James that a prayer of faith will save the sick and if the person has committed any sins, then these will be forgiven him.[167] Jesus actually demonstrated the healing of the soul and the healing of the physical body when the paralysed man was let down on his bed by his four friends through the roof so that Jesus could heal him. First Jesus healed the man of his sins and then He healed him so he could walk.[168]

God doesn't change. Since Jesus came from God and was the one through whom all things were created, He can't change either. He healed everybody who came to Him. One leper came to Him and asked the question that is so often on our unbelieving lips: "Lord, if You are willing, You can make me clean," and Jesus "Put out His hand and touched him, saying, 'I am willing; be cleansed.'"[169]

Jesus is the same as He was yesterday. He will be the same

---

[167] James 5:14-16
[168] Luke 5:17-39
[169] Matt 8:2-3

tomorrow. He is willing to heal all who turn to Him in faith and trust. Remember, you only need a mustard seed's worth of faith and you only need a breadcrumb of Jesus' body to be healed.

## Chapter 16
# The Cancer Has Gone!

*"Bless the LORD, O my soul; and all that is within me, bless His holy name! Bless the LORD, O my soul, and forget not all His benefits: Who forgives all your iniquities, Who heals all your diseases ... Who satisfies your mouth with good things, so that your youth is renewed like the eagle's."*
(Psalm 103:1-3, 5)

In July 2019 we were meeting with a little group of non-denominational faithful Christians who believed in the power of the Holy Spirit to heal. It was amongst them that I revealed that I had cancer and I would like prayer for healing. I totally believed that this would be the moment I would be healed completely of my cancer and I told them so.

It's strange to say this, but the cancer was beginning to feel like something that had happened in another lifetime to another person. It wasn't that I denied that I had been diagnosed as having cancer, it was more that the cancer was irrelevant to me. It was all about God and His sole ability to save. The more I turned to God, the more the cancer became distanced from me.

When I was prayed for I felt super-charged energy surge through me — the power, δύναμιν, the "dunamis", the "dynamite" of the Holy Spirit. There was no doubt in my mind that I was healed in that instant. The group all started prophesying over me and confirmed that I had indeed been healed. Praise God! We all thanked God together. I fully believed I was healed. There wasn't a shred of doubt in my mind.

Two days later I went for a CT scan to restage my metastatic breast cancer. I received the CT scan results before my sixth round of chemo. My oncologist came in to see me, smiling and excited. There wasn't any sign of the cancer. I was informed that the lung nodules were stable and were almost certainly post-inflammatory. (It was explained to me later that you can't have cancerous nodes on the lungs and not have scars remaining.) My oncologist confessed that the research didn't support this outcome and she wasn't sure what should be done next. She asked my permission to confer with other oncologists to determine the pathway forward.

In the end it was decided to continue the chemo for a total of nine rounds and to continue with the three weekly targeted drugs, Perjeta and Herceptin, indefinitely. Until I had a PET scan, which was scheduled for January, the medical teams could only assume that all the cancer had gone, but as far as I was concerned, God had banished that cancer from my body.

I went back to my little group and announced that there was no sign of the cancer and we all thanked and praised God for His kindness and mercy to me.

Other CT scans and mammograms have since confirmed that there is no sign of any cancer and my oncologist has told me that I am in the unique and "enviable position" to consider discontinuation of therapy altogether. I'm letting the medical team make those decisions because the targeted treatment has no ill effects on me and I want to have my healing fully documented.

After another CT scan in October 2020 that again confirmed that the cancer had indeed gone, my oncologist remarked to me that she has read the literature about HER2 positive cancer, the different treatments, the outcomes and current research into this cancer and that nowhere has there been a single case of a person being cured of HER2. As far as she knows I am the only person in the world to have been actually cured of this particular cancer. Praise God!

## Chapter 17
# The Power of His Resurrection

*"(I want to know Christ) and the power of His resurrection and the fellowship of His sufferings, being conformed to His death."*
(Phil 3:10)

In his unsaved days, my husband, Pete, had traversed the world looking for the meaning of life. He had meditated in the Mahabodhi Temple Complex of Bodh Gaya in India where Gautama Buddha is said to have attained enlightenment. Sitting there in a lotus position doing his pranayama breathing, inspired by magic mushrooms and mesmerised by chanting and percussion instruments, he felt euphoric and often on the verge of enlightenment.

After such an exalted experience, he sensed he had reached the zenith of humanity's existence. From there he went on to work in Iran for a few months and thereafter returned to the lure of India. This time, however, he found the enlightenment experience had nothing more to offer him and he perceived a strong urge to continue his search for the meaning of life in Perth.

It was on his second day in Perth that he met an old friend from NZ who told him his life had been transformed by Jesus, even changing his name from Brian to Joshua, a form of Jesus. He invited Pete to dinner in a house where he lived with a group of Christians and after much discussion and debate Pete was challenged to pray to receive Jesus as his Saviour. His prayer was answered supernaturally and he felt the tangible presence of Jesus on him and the Fatherhood of God and in one fell swoop he knew that he had finally found the meaning of life.

All the philosophies and religions of this world teach us to rise to a higher version of ourselves. The Gospel not only does not teach us to rise, but shows us we are utterly incapable of doing anything good in and of ourselves. It teaches that when we surrender to the reality of Jesus we can be born again from above and sustained by heavenly powers.

The Christian life is not a self-development course as many people mistakenly think it is, but rather it is a supernatural and divine experience that draws us into a close and intimate relationship with the Creator of the entire universe. The less you value your own righteousness the more you will seek true holiness. The more you give up trying to save yourself, the more productive you will become in showing the fruits of the Spirit.

Resurrection is the foundation of our Christian faith. The resurrection is proof that Jesus really did conquer the power of death, that Satan really was defeated, that our sins were fully dealt with and that we can hope to be resurrected and live with Christ forever.

The power of the resurrection is that Jesus lives. Jesus lives to pardon us of all our sins, to heal us, to intercede for us. Jesus lives to make us whole. Jesus has paid the penalty for all our wrongs and he was discharged because He had satisfied the claim of the law. "The soul who sins shall die"[170] and Jesus paid that price for sinners like you and me. He was our substitute. He took on all the punishment that was our due and he rose again from the dead for our justification for Jesus "Is the end of the law for righteousness to everyone who believes."[171]

Not only were we pardoned, but we have been "accepted in the Beloved."[172] The resurrection is a guarantee that you have been pardoned, justified and accepted. I hope that knowing that you are now a part of the body of Christ because of His resurrection will bring you joy knowing you are known, beloved and delighted in by the Lord God.

---

[170] Ezek. 18:20
[171] Rom. 10:4
[172] Eph. 1:6

When one sinner turns to God the angels of God are joyful and delighted[173] and there is a most beautiful picture in the Bible of how much God delights in you and rejoices over you when you turn to Jesus and let your old self be crucified with Him.[174] It's found in Zephaniah. God had ended His judgment on "filthy and polluted" Israel leading up to the time for God to be joyful because the relationship with Israel had been restored and Jesus was reigning: "Yahweh your God is in your midst, a victorious warrior. He will exult with joy over you, He will renew you by His love; He will dance with shouts of joy for you as on a day of festival."[175]

Can you picture this? Almighty God, the God who created the entire universe, is not the quiet and dignified being that so many portray Him as, nor is He observing us from a distance, but He is deeply emotional, exuberantly shouting in joy over the restoration of the bonds of love. Our God celebrates and hollers with delight over us because of the miraculous, inexplicable forgiveness of our "filth and pollution" when God, Himself, paid the price for our redemption and His relationship with us was restored.

---

173  Luke 15:10
174  Rom. 6:6
175  Zeph. 3:17-18 (Jer. Bib).

## Chapter 18
# Who Gets Custody of Your Emotional Health?

*"He heals the brokenhearted
and binds up their wounds."*
(Psalm 147:3)

My Muslim associates in Iran were amazed that I had had an upbringing in my teenage years that was akin to theirs — some even found that my upbringing had been even more restrictive than theirs. Anyone living in a legalistic, male-dominated culture will understand what my life had been like. The cult had instilled a lot of negativity by its strange practices and insistence on upholding so many standards.

I have heard that on the day that my father's parents were baptised into the cult, when my father was about 12 years old, my grandparents had suddenly closed their door to their neighbours with whom they had always enjoyed weekly card games and games of tennis in the backyard and my grandparents refused to associate with them ever again. Association with non-Christadelphians is very much frowned upon, but I wonder what their perplexed and bewildered neighbours must have thought when they found their doors tightly closed without any explanation.

I once chanced upon a third cousin on my mother's side who was not a part of the cult and he related how when my maternal great grandfather had joined the cult, he had immediately severed all ties with his own family, much to their sorrow and bafflement. It was very interesting for me to hear how my cast-off family members viewed the ones who had severed them off as having acted superior, haughty and opinionated.

My finishing Year 12 had been frowned upon in the religious group, but later when it became known that I was attending university, I was openly criticised, reprimanded and castigated for pursuing the so-called "wisdom of this world". I was frequently told I had a bad attitude for wanting to pursue education and was referred to as the one who was rejecting Jesus' wisdom for that of the world.

On top of that I was married to a fellow Christadelphian who, many years later, was involved with my close friend. I was in very deep anguish and heartache. I felt utterly worthless and ugly. I was crushed, broken, bruised and bleeding. I just wanted to die.

Divorce was inevitable, but my biggest fear through all of this was that I would end up as a resentful, man-hating divorcee mistrustful of all women — having a "root of bitterness"[176] that the devil could seize, manipulate and use to contaminate others to become morally defiled. I prayed fervently night and day that God would forgive the pair who had betrayed me and that God would keep my spirit sweet. I really meant it. My relationship with God depended on it. Kingdom life and power flowing in my life depended on it.

If ever there was a time in my life that I needed a constant reminder that God was for me and not against me it was then. I was fully aware that our battle is not against flesh and blood, that people are not the enemy so I knew I had to keep focussed on God, no matter what. The root of all evil is the devil and he uses people and circumstances to turn us away from God. I was so broken inside I couldn't think clearly, but I had enough clarity to fix my eyes on this affirmation:

> You are not unwanted. You are chosen.
> You are not unloved. You were to die for.
> You are not alone. You are His.

I added an image of these words as my phone screensaver so it was ever in front of my face. I regularly read those words

---

[176] Heb. 12:15. Incidentally, the Greek word for "the many" is "hoi polloi", a term we've borrowed for use in English.

out loud. I was so struggling with despair that all I could do was stammer out to God, "Help me."

Friends gave me a personalised magic mug that lit up when heated with these very words so my mind was constantly bombarded with the truth that I was special to God. I forced myself to meditate on the journey of my life of being found by God, the wonderful experiences God had blessed me with in the Holy Spirit, the people who had come to Jesus because of me and the huge crowd of witnesses in the heavenlies who were cheering me on.

I read the messages of love scattered throughout the Bible. For example, just look at how the word for "given" (Greek δέδωκεν (dedōken)) has been used in merely one small book in the Bible, encouraging us that God has gifted us, lavished us, with His love, His Spirit and understanding:

"See what great love the Father has lavished on us, that we should be called children of God! And that is what we are!"[177]

"By this we know that we abide in Him, and He in us, because He has given us of His Spirit."[178]

"And we know that the Son of God has come and has given

---

[177] 1 John 3:1 (NIV)
[178] 1 John 4:13

us an understanding, that we may know Him who is true; and we are in Him who is true, in His Son Jesus Christ. This is the true God and eternal life."[179]

I listened to praise music. At every big upheaval in my life there has been a musical genre that I have turned to to lift my spirits. I can't really explain the rationale, but different genres have spoken to me at different times. At this stage in my life, I turned to quiet and pensive Christian songs to hear positive messages over and over again.

I continuously focussed on the joy of being in Christ, but for a time it didn't feel like anything was changing. I knew that if your mind is stayed on Jesus as your rock and anchor Satan can't take advantage of your situation and accuse you so that you take your eyes off your Heavenly Father and instead focus on your problems and yourself. It really was a battle to keep myself focussed on God being all loving, all powerful and all providing and not sink into self-pity. It took everything in me to put God above my problems.

Apart from healing for the cancer, I desperately needed healing from my own emotional pain. It took a lot of counselling and reading to realise I had been identifying myself with this emotional pain and physical illness. I'd been acting act out of fear, anger, defensiveness and

---

[179] 1 John 5:20

judgment and even though I wanted to emanate love and joy and be open to all human beings, I couldn't. I kept on unconsciously resisting or sabotaging any and every attempt to heal that pain.

Pete was just amazing. He helped me to know what was going on in my head and wouldn't let the pain overtake my mind and thinking. He led me to a place of acceptance so that I was released from needing to control everything around me and to let go of my fear. He helped me to forgive the past and to allow the present moment to be. Above all he prayed continually with me.

One day in our little group of Christians as we prayed for one another, we prayed against anything that was blocking us going forward with Jesus. I asked for prayer, but I didn't say what the prayer was for — that was between God and me. I wanted to place all my brokenness and pain at the foot of the cross. When the Holy Spirit came on me on that occasion, I felt an incredibly strong blast of power overwhelm me — like I would imagine being hit by lightning would feel like. Even when I had been prayed for to be healed of the cancer, it had been a less strong touch of the Holy Spirit.

With such a strong presence of God on me, I had no doubt I had been healed of all my emotional pain. In truth, I didn't feel any differently at the time (except for a few hours afterwards when I had an aching and spinning head from that massive charge of power), but in the course of life I realised that all my fears and pains had gone. I was free. No longer was there any hurt or anguish remaining in me. My emotional pain no longer owned me.

I had proven that on my own I couldn't fight the grief, despair, fear and loneliness, but when I had surrendered myself to God it had all been dissolved. God had straightforwardly taken over and done what I couldn't do and was making me a new person in Christ Jesus. In surrendering to Jesus I had come to the realisation that the past was powerless. I understood that nothing I ever did or was done to me could mar the fact that I was a chosen child of God, worthy of His love and salvation. The past had ceased to have any power.

Declaring who you are in Jesus is a powerful weapon against Satan. When you become a true believer in Jesus, you are born into the family of God and out of the family of Satan. From then on, Satan will do everything in his power to bring Christians down and back into his camp. One of his best tactics that has successfully destroyed Christians is to get Christians to dwell on their failures and to guilt trip them into weakness and helplessness.

Satan doesn't want you to know that God does not punish those who trust in Him. Satan doesn't want you to read the story of Peter's restoration after his monumental failure in denying Jesus. That's right — God does not get even because you have sinned. God has already dealt with Jesus for all of our sins: past, present and even future sins. God loves you unconditionally, which is why He sent Jesus to die for you.

The sad truth is that we have all sinned and come short of the glory of God[180], but Jesus died for all sinners.[181]. The very fact that Jesus is in heaven today is proof that He bore all your sins on the tree[182] and not one of your sins remain, no matter how big that sin has been. If a single sin had remained, Jesus would still be here on earth because it says: "He was delivered up because of our offenses, and was raised because of our justification. Therefore, having been justified by faith, we have peace with God through our Lord Jesus Christ."[183] All we need to do is "confess our sins, (for) He is faithful and just to forgive us our sins and cleanse us from all unrighteousness."[184]

God has a plan for your life and He will take everything that has happened to you, whether that has been good or bad, and He will make it all work together for your good.[185]

---

180  Rom. 3:23
181  Rom. 5:8
182  1 Pet. 2:24
183  Rom. 4:25; 5:1.
184  1 John 1:9
185  Rom. 8:28

In Revelation 12:11 we are told that the Christians overcame and conquered Satan because of the blood of the Lamb and because of the word of their faithful testimony even when faced with death. The bad things in your life, then, must work out to be a means of blessing you. You know God is not bringing trials on you to punish you so he must be allowing these trials to come on you as part of His overall plan to bless your life. When you understand this you are able, in the midst of trials, to praise God for the trial. There is power in your praise.

If you think you have problems, let's revisit Jehoshaphat, the king of Judah again. He was told that a great multitude of nations were on their way to fight against him and his kingdom. These armies wanted to wipe them out to the very last man and Jehoshaphat had only just barely escaped death from an earlier battle and he was terrified. He gathered all the people of Judah together and asked for help from God. He publicly admitted that Judah was defenceless against the armies coming against them and that their only means of victory was through God.

A prophet in the midst of all the assembled people spontaneously prophesied that the battle was not Jehoshaphat's but God's. Jehoshaphat was told not to be afraid but to go down against them, to set up as if they were going into battle and watch the God of armies vindicate them.

In faith, the next day Jehoshaphat and Judah headed out against the vast armies arrayed against them and Jehoshaphat urged the people, as they were going on their way, to believe in the Lord and believe His prophets and so they would prosper. He got the appointed singers to lead the way singing aloud, "Praise the Lord, for His mercy endures forever."

Don't just read those verses glibly! Jehoshaphat was facing the battle of his life and they were heading out for battle yet he put the defenceless Levites at the helm to lead the way. Think about what faith that must have taken for Jehoshaphat to do that! (On that score, I think it must have taken a lot of faith to be a Levite in that situation, singing confidently and playing their stringed instruments, harps and trumpets with hordes of battle-hardened soldiers wielding their weapons laying in wait for them.) The Bible says:

"Now when they began to sing and to praise, the Lord set ambushes against the people of Ammon, Moab, and Mount Seir, who had come against Judah; and they were defeated."[186]

When Judah got to a spot overlooking the multitude, there were dead bodies scattered far and wide and Jehoshaphat and Judah rejoiced and blessed the name of God. (I expect

---

[186] 2 Chron. 20:22

they were doubly joyful because the Bible records that it took them 3 days to strip all the jewellery and valuables that were on the dead bodies.)

Being fearful, terrified and threatened is not a block to seeing the power of God rising in your situation. No barrier on earth exists that can keep you from Jesus' love for you and your restoration. Here is the secret of power against emotional distress: the power of steadfast and unshakeable belief in God to restore and heal. When you have that confidence in your Healer, you can't but help praising and worshipping Him.

This may sound strange, but to me, healing from emotional pain was a far, far, far greater miracle than healing from the cancer. With healing from emotional pain, I feel that I am a new creation and that fact just fills me with love and gratitude to my Saviour who paid such a price for me to be made whole. To anyone reading this who is suffering from deep emotional scars, know that when you surrender yourself entirely to Jesus there can be complete peace and freedom in this life.

We are warned to keep our hearts with all diligence for out of the heart spring the issues of life.[187] In other words, our hearts are the centre for everything in our lives; our lives

---

187  Prov. 4:23

flow from our hearts. If our inner being has been crushed, then the person with a wounded spirit will hobble through life. This is not the state of affairs that God planned for His children and it is not the outcome for a faithful Christian who trusts in Jesus as His Healer.

I used to teach large classes of new Christian converts and I encountered so much brokenness in people. One day I said that we ALL need Jesus. We are ALL broken and I had every person in that room nodding their heads in agreement. We all come to Jesus with baggage for Him to heal.

We are surrounded by pain. I have a movie producer friend who once said to me that life takes us down dark paths and that artists use devastating events to share the common human experience. My Kurdish friend writes the most incredible poetry in which he uses figurative language so beautifully that he captures the pain of torture and death. We relate because we are human. We all know what it is like to have pain in our lives.

What sort of things happen to people that they feel that they must conceal weapons under their jackets and go about the streets looking tough? Or worse, use those weapons and kill people? Or sink into male prostitution? Or grapple with addictions to sex, drugs or alcohol? I've heard it all and I've seen people healed. God is faithful to the one who turns to Him.

Brokenness can beset us for life from even seemingly innocuous little events that happen to us. One man had been going through life unable to keep a job or stay in a relationship because of one little event in his life. He privately confessed to me that as a young man he had been drinking in a pub and as one of his mates left he had carelessly called out, "God bless you, bro" and the man went outside and was hit by a truck and killed. He truly believed he had cursed that man and caused his death! He carried that pain all his life.

For my part, I pointed out that he had unwittingly pronounced a blessing on that man and that the last words that poor man had heard were words of hope and who knows if, in that flash of time, his words had turned that man's heart to Jesus? I explained that there would have been no better words to say to a man immediately before his death than "God bless you, bro."

The man had a revelation about himself that day. We prayed and the man was released from his lifelong pain. This is just what the Bible promised.

So many times in the Bible it had been prophesied in the Old Testament that Jesus would rain righteousness or bring showers of blessing with His appearance. For instance, Psalm 72:6 says Jesus will come down like "Rain upon the grass before mowing, Like showers that water the earth."

Just like our bodies need feeding, so too does our spirit and this picture of refreshing rain from Jesus showering down on us and reviving our spirits, taking away all the dryness in our souls, the withered and wasted thought patterns, the wilted and parched hope in our hearts, the aridity of our lives is why Jesus is said to bring invigorating and revitalising refreshment into our spirits.

The healing from emotional pain is just one of those blessings that Jesus has rained upon us. Acts 3:19-20 in the Amplified Bible has: "So repent (change your inner self — your old way of thinking, regret past sins) and return (to God — seek His presence for your life), so that your sins may be wiped away (blotted out, completely erased), so that times of refreshing may come from the presence of the Lord (restoring you like a cool wind on a hot day); and that He may send (to you) Jesus, the Christ, who has been appointed for you." What a promise we have when we repent and turn to Jesus! When we do come to Jesus and turn over to Him our anguish and hurt, then we can be completely sustained and nourished to wholeness.

It is up to us to receive that blessing or not. We can choose to have the Spirit of God breathing life into our thirsty souls — the Spirit is just waiting there for anyone to come to Jesus for refreshment. This is what Jesus promised: "On the last day, that great day of the feast, Jesus stood and cried out, saying, 'If anyone thirsts, let him come to Me and drink. He who believes in Me, as the Scripture has said, out of his heart will flow rivers of living water.' But this He spoke concerning the Spirit, whom those believing in Him should receive; for the Holy Spirit was not yet given, because Jesus was not yet glorified."[188] By acknowledging our thirst, our hurts and distress, and turning to Jesus for revival, then we can be given healing waters from the throne room of God to be blessed beyond measure. Once we are healed the blessings of the Spirit will emanate from us towards others.

The Bible has many verses to describe what it feels like to have your spirit broken. Verses like "By sorrow of the heart the spirit is broken"[189] and "A broken spirit dries the bones"[190] describe what it is like when a person is damaged in their spirit and can't keep it together when the slightest of physical troubles or upsets affect them. There is a proverb that says that when we lose control of our spirit we are like a city without walls that has been broken down[191]. When we have been betrayed, failed or had our trust broken, we are vulnerable to losing control of our spirit, and when that happens we are defenceless against the attacks of the devil.

When we are washed with the Spirit's waters, God

---

188  John 7:37-39
189  Prov. 15:13
190  Prov. 17:22
191  Prov. 25:28

will restore all that we have ever lost. There is hope for restoration beyond that which we had started out with if we allow the Holy Spirit to come inside us to heal us. Like Job who lost everything when he was afflicted by Satan and then had everything restored to him doubly over, so you, too, can expect to have restored to you that which has been lost to you. I know because that is what God has promised!

Remember in Acts how the disciples were gathered together on the day of Pentecost and the Spirit touched them all with what looked like tongues of fire? The disciples then started speaking in other tongues and everyone was confounded and thought they must be drunk before Peter stood up and said that this was what had been promised by God that in the latter days He would pour out His Spirit on all flesh? Peter said that this promise (of receiving the Holy Spirit after repenting and being baptised in the name of Jesus for the remission of sins) was for "You, to your children, and to all who are afar off, as many as the Lord our God will call."[192]

If we head back to Joel 2 where this promise was first made, we read that because of the rains to be poured out on God's people, they would never be "ashamed", the same root word that is used of Adam and Eve after creation when they were naked and not ashamed. It is sin that has brought shame,

---

[192] Acts 2:38-39

humiliation, anguish and pain, but it is God's Spirit sent to us because of what Jesus did that will bring us peace and contentment.

Let's read Joel 2:23-27 because it reinforces what we can expect from God: "Be glad then, you children of Zion, and rejoice in the LORD your God, for He has given you the former rain faithfully, and He will cause the rain to come down for you — the former rain and the latter rain in the first month. The threshing floors shall be full of wheat, and the vats shall overflow with new wine and oil. So I will restore to you the years that the swarming locust has eaten, the crawling locust, the consuming locust, and the chewing locust, My great army which I sent among you. You shall eat in plenty and be satisfied, and praise the name of the LORD your God Who has dealt wondrously with you; and My people shall never be put to shame. Then you shall know that I am in the midst of Israel: I am the LORD your God and there is no other. My people shall never be put to shame."

My undergraduate studies included a year studying climatology. After graduation for a short while I ended up as a high school teacher with the unenviable task of making sense of the different climates of the world to a classroom full of hormonal teenagers who wanted nothing more than to escape school and have fun. In order to get something through to their largely unreceptive minds, I reduced the climates of the world to simple phrases. In the case of the climate of biblical countries, the Mediterranean climate, I had the classes repeating: "summer drought — winter rain". So what's the relevance of that here?

What we have here is God saying that after the long dry summer, the first rains would start in the autumn, around October, when the seed was planted and the rains would keep on raining right through to the spring in the first month, referred to as the last rains, which occurred around March or April, when the crops would start to be reaped and harvested.

As a result of those rains the people would be abundantly blessed with overflowing vats and barns so that any onlooker would know that God had blessed His people. Everything that God's people had lost in the past would be restored.

We know from the context in Acts that rains refer to the outpouring of the Holy Spirit so we have Joel here foretelling an outpouring of the Holy Spirit that would bring abundant blessings and that this outpouring would continue with great signs and wonders until the great and awesome day of the Lord arrives.[193] As God's people living in the age after the Holy Spirit started to be poured

---
[193] Joel 2:29-31

out on the earth, we have been showered with blessing after blessing through the Holy Spirit to free us from sin, physical pain, emotional pain and demonic oppression. What a lovely Father!

"The righteous cry out, and the Lord hears, and delivers them out of all their troubles. The Lord is near to those who have a broken heart, and saves such as have a contrite spirit. Many are the afflictions of the righteous, but the Lord delivers him out of them all. He guards all his bones; not one of them is broken."[194]

How true that God watches over us and guards even our bones! The truth of those words was about to be made abundantly clear to me, as I relate another incident in my cancer journey.

---

194  Psa. 34:17-20

# Chapter 19

# The Worst — Losing Hair and Losing LOTS of Hair

> *"Are not two sparrows sold for a copper coin? And not one of them falls to the ground apart from your Father's will. But the very hairs of your head are all numbered. Do not fear therefore; you are of more value than many sparrows."*
>
> **(Matt. 10:29-31)**

In the whole of my episode with cancer, it was the loss of my hair that alarmed me the most. I hadn't lost any significant amount of hair on my head during my cold-capping time, but two months afterwards my scalp had what is termed, "chemical burning", and my hair was falling out in distressingly large handfuls. At any single time I could collect handfuls of hair just by gently pulling on the ends of my hair and those handfuls translated into full plastic bags. I can't tell you how disturbing that experience was for me. Pete helpfully suggested that we could use it for stuffing a cushion or even to spin it to make clothing! Going days without touching my hair left me starting to look like the Wild Woman of Borneo and so I took to wearing hats, turbans, cloches, scarves, berets, Persian hijabs — anything to cover that thinning hair.

I naturally have a lot more hair than most people so even with the huge loss of hair I was able to still look like I had a normal head of hair, but people who knew me noticed. One of my daughters commented that she had never seen me with such thin hair. My hairdresser reassured me I had a normal amount of hair, but that didn't console me. I knew what was happening.

I constantly asked the day clinic staff and my oncologist for answers, but no answers were given. It was hard for them to actually appreciate the extent of my hair loss because my head of hair didn't exactly look abnormal. My oncologist told me that she believed that the hair loss was the delayed effects of chemo because chemo stays in the body long after treatment has ended.

In desperation I asked Pete and another member of our group to pray for my hair to return. I felt vain and self-centred, but that didn't stop me asking God for a miracle. I didn't feel any differently after the prayer, but two weeks later I noticed little sprouts of regrowth all around my face. Three months later I could hardly believe it when my hairdresser advised me that my hair needed thinning out as it was far too thick! She didn't trim the length, just thinned it out. Six weeks after that extensive hair thinning, my hairdresser advised again that my hair didn't need trimming, but it did need even further thinning out!

I learnt the lesson in this that God actually deeply cares about the things that we care about, that nothing is too small or trivial to ask God for help with. Further, I learnt that God really does number the very hairs on our head and tends us as a loving Father answering the needs of His loved child. God is ever ready to listen to our pleas when we are overwhelmed. Just hand your burdens, anxieties and cares over to the Lord, no matter how inconsequential and insignificant, and He will sustain you.[195] Losing hair may not seem like much of a burden to you, but it was to me, and therefore it was to God.

---

[195] Psa. 55:22; I Pet. 5:7; Matt. 11:28-30.

## Chapter 20
# The Power of Prayer for a Husband

*"Therefore I say to you, whatever things you ask when you pray, believe that you receive them, and you will have them."*
(Mark 11:24)

I had been left single and was on the road to recovery from the trauma of my ex-husband and friend betraying me, when the next chapter in my life was opening. I was living by myself and feeling so desperately lonely. I had good, loving and supportive friends, but it was the lonely trip to church each Sunday that I found unbearable. Going home one Sunday I was in tears and said to God that I didn't think I could go to church alone any more.

On the basis that we have not because we don't ask, I asked God to find me a partner that week — and I dared to ask for three things as a sign that he was God sent. I had made a bad judgment the last time and this time I wanted it to be solely God's decision. Firstly, he had to be Biblically literate — a genuine and secure Christian with a stable personality. Secondly, he had to have worked in Iran. That's a strange request, but I had spent time working there in 2011 and I had been forever changed as a result. Unless you have lived in Iran you wouldn't know why I loved the place, people, food and culture so much, and understand the extreme difficulties that Christians there experience. I needed someone who could appreciate that significant part of who I was. Thirdly, I asked for a man who could sail. I liked the way sailors are team players and were generally calm people — probably more an idealisation in my head than a reality, but at the time it was important. I had also said to God that if he chose not to provide me with a partner, I would accept that and not ask again. He heard my prayer and answered it extraordinarily.

It was in the following week that I first saw Pete's face and distinctly heard God saying, "This is the man I've chosen for you." It's a really strange experience to be looking at someone you know nothing about yet knowing that that was the man God had handpicked for you and that you would be marrying that person.

And did God meet my conditions? What do you think? Pete had been a Christian pastor and had pioneered churches in Australia and New Zealand. He had been an avid Bible student and had a wealth of Biblical knowledge and experience. He is a rock of a person who you can rely on for help and support and he had a happy, consistent and balanced personality. In a strange twist of fate he had actually witnessed the Gospel to my former parents-in-law in New Zealand. In another very strange twist of fate, he had been at the very first church service I had ever attended, nearly 20 years ago.

On the second condition: Pete, in his youth, had worked for the Imperial Iranian Navy under the Shah, teaching English to naval cadets in Rasht, Iran. In 2005 he had returned for a quick visit to deliver Bibles to Christians there.

On the third count, Pete had sailed the Mediterranean, Atlantic and Pacific.

God had answered my prayer to find me a husband who was almost a complete mirror of all my deepest thoughts and philosophies, with the same unique sense of humour and quirkiness.

I'd heard about God selecting partners for people before, which is why I asked God. I have a friend in Sweden who was working in Israel and she was told by God to return to Sweden to attend a church conference where she would meet her future husband. A Swedish man, unknown to her, was also working in another part of Israel and he was also told by God to also attend the same conference in Sweden where he would meet his future wife. When my friend was standing in the doorway to the conference centre in Sweden, her future husband was told by God to turn around in his seat to see his future wife in the doorway. They have now been happily married for decades.

I knew another man whose first wife had died of cystic fibrosis. When he had recovered from her death and felt ready, he had asked God for a wife. As his first wife had been blonde he dared to ask for a redhead this time. The following week God introduced him to his lovely redhead.

When you think about it, it's not that strange that God selects partners for us because even Abraham trusted in God to provide a partner for his son when he sent his servant far away to the land of his relatives to fetch a wife for Isaac. Abraham assured his servant that God's angel would lead him and we have the record that when the servant had arrived in the area and was resting beside a spring, he prayed to God that if he approached a young lady for a drink of water and she offered him a drink for his camels also, then this would be the sign that this was the wife God had chosen for Isaac. And so Isaac trusted God to choose his companion for life and be the mother of God's future Israel, Rebekah.[196]

Our wedding day, on a perfect spring day, was set in a surf lifesaving clubhouse overlooking a beach that we regularly

---

[196] You can read about it in Genesis 24.

walk along. It was an unforgettable day. As we were being married and afterwards, humpback whales were leaping out of the sparkling blue water behind us, frolicking in the brilliant sunshine. It was a God blessed moment.

For 43 long and painful years I had prayed daily that my husband would one day love me and that he would have time for me. Here I am today with God having answered that prayer in a way I could never have envisaged and having blessed me with a husband who does love and protect me like no other, a man who speaks words of tenderness and encouragement to me every single day. When Pete told me that he would count it as an enormous privilege to have me beside him for the rest of his life and that I would never leave his heart, not even for a second, I knew that this sweet man was going to be here to romance me forever. In Pete, my prayer for a loyal, loving and attentive husband has been answered in spades.

We sometimes tend to take our life for granted, our health and the meaning of life, forgetting that "in Him we live and move and have our being."[197] God wants to provide for us in all areas of our life and that verse has such intensity and implications when we ponder its meaning. It means that if our life is bound with God's life, we have life, we have vitality, we have meaning to that life, we have a reason for

---
197  Acts 17:28

existence, we have joy and happiness in that life and we can also expect to have health. Specifically, for me, having been given a metastatic cancer diagnosis with a miserable prognosis, that meant I could expect my upcoming PET scan to show no sign of cancer.

## Chapter 21
# The PET Scan Confirms the Cancer Has Gone

*"Now this is the confidence that we have in Him, that if we ask anything according to His will, He hears us. And if we know that He hears us, whatever we ask, we know that we have the petitions that we have asked of Him."*
(1 John 5:14-15)

My normally sober oncologist was elated when I arrived for my appointment with her in February. In late January 2020 I had had the long-anticipated PET scan to conclusively confirm that my cancer had indeed gone.

As my oncologist ushered me into her room she exclaimed, "Great results" and she went on to read out the long report. To put it sketchily, there was now no sign of cancer anywhere — specifically that there had been a "Complete metabolic response with resolution of FDG avid right axillary nodes, post-surgical changes at the primary site and resolution of FDG avid pulmonary nodules."

She impressed on me that you never see these kinds of results with HER2 positive cancer. I had been first diagnosed with breast cancer in April 2019; had had surgery to remove the two lumps and lymph nodes in May 2019; in July 2019 the CT scan, after five rounds of chemo, had shown the cancer had gone (pending the January PET scan to confirm that the "spots" on my lungs really were scars and not cancerous nodes); had had nine rounds of chemotherapy that concluded in August 2019, and now here was the ultimate proof that the cancer had wholly been resolved. Praise God, Yahweh Rapha, God my Healer!

When I went into the day clinic to receive the routinely scheduled targeted therapy every staff member greeted me warmly and congratulated me. Apparently my oncologist had called them to a team meeting before I had arrived to tell them the good news. Over and over again it was confirmed to me that they never see this sort of thing.

My oncologist told me recently that I was in the "enviable position" of revisiting the necessity for that treatment protocol in a year's time so, for the time being, I am happy to continue having my regular drug cocktails. Meanwhile, I get to speak with other people who are battling cancer every time I attend the clinic and can tell them about a God who saves us from sin and heals us of our diseases.

On one occasion I was hooked up and sitting in the day

clinic with everyone around me hooked up to their drug infusions. The lady opposite started chatting and asked me what sort of cancer did I have? I replied that I had had breast cancer, but it was all gone.

She replied how lucky I was and that her cancer had gone to her lymph nodes. I replied that I also had had cancer in my lymph nodes.

She reiterated that the medical team must've caught it early because her cancer had metastasised to her lungs and that there wasn't any hope for her. I told her that mine had, too.

At this stage she was looking at me as though I was telling the most enormous lies she had ever heard. She then informed me that she was in Stage IV — that hers was incurable and she only had months to live. I told her that I had been in Stage IV and I had also been told that I had only six months to live if I had been untreated and possibly as long as 18 months with treatment and that my cancer was incurable.

It was now all too much for this poor lady and she called over the nurse attending us both and asked, "This lady says she had Stage IV cancer and now it has all gone." The nurse replied, "Yes. That's true. Wonderful isn't it!"

Now the lady was ready to hear what was different about

my cancer journey to have such an amazing outcome. She asked me, "What did you do to get yourself healed? Did you change your diet? Did you get into yoga and meditation? Did you use any special supplements?"

I replied that I simply believed in Jesus as my Healer. Just as He healed 2,000 years ago, He wants to heal today. Believe in Him as your Saviour and all His blessings will come to you when you totally trust in Him.

As I drew breath to tell her more, her eyes glazed over and she slunk down in her reclining chair. "I'm not into that kind of stuff and not interested." Like the two thieves on the cross breathing their final breaths, one thief turned to Jesus and the other condemned Jesus. Not even Jesus had all people responding to His message of freedom and blessing and all we can do is tell people about Jesus and the amazing blessings that He offers them at no cost.

How sad is it that even when people are in their greatest time of need of a Saviour, they refuse to come to Him and ask. I find that incredible and pray that people's hearts will turn to the most loving friend they will ever encounter and that their lives will be transformed as a result.

Hurt, broken and suffering people are everywhere around us. God will use anyone who believes in Him to reach them and bring them to Him as their Saviour.

There once was a British pastor from the 19th century, Joseph Parker, who counselled would-be preachers to "Speak to the suffering, you will never lack an audience. There is a broken heart in every crowd."[198] Grief, heartache, pain and loss are common for all humanity.

Jesus declared that His mission on earth was to set wretched and lost captives free,[199] people who have been imprisoned unwittingly by the arch-enemy, Satan. Jesus, in His day, was absurdly but blasphemously accused of healing people by the power of "Beelzebub, the ruler of the demons"[200] yet it was this very Jesus, who came from the Father's heart to meet this strong man and crush him underfoot. After dying on the cross and rising again to eternal life, we have proof that Jesus completely rendered the devil powerless and opened the door for us to be with Him for eternity: "If the Spirit of Him who raised Jesus from the dead dwells in you, He who raised Christ from the dead will also give life to your mortal bodies through His Spirit who dwells in you."[201]

All that is required is for the captives, in their own time and space, to pray to Jesus with their whole heart. The leper came to Jesus as a leper. The blind man came to Jesus as a

---

198 https://www.azquotes.com/quote/1425648 accessed 7.10.20
199 Luke 4:18
200 Luke 11:15
201 Rom. 8:11

blind man. The crazed man in the tombs came to Jesus as a madman. You can come to Jesus how you are and wherever you are by simply praying from your heart:

Father, I come to you as a sinner. I need forgiveness. Please forgive me for all my sins. I turn to Jesus. I believe that Jesus died on the cross and paid the price for my sin. I receive Jesus as my Lord and Saviour I thank you for this incredible gift of salvation and I give myself completely for His glory, to serve You, to love You and to obey You for the rest of my life. Amen.

I want to now elaborate what saying that "Amen" means.

# Chapter 22
# The Power of Your Amen

*"For all the promises of God in Him are Yes, and in Him Amen, to the glory of God through us."*
(2 Cor. 1:20)

This section could have also been termed "The power of your confession" or "The power of your positive assertion" because this is the meaning of the word "Amen". After Christians pray, those who agree with the words of the prayer will say aloud, "Amen" — verily, truly, let it be true, so be it, let it be so. After you have made a petition to God, you have asserted to and agreed that this is what you confidently expect will happen.

Actually, this principle of confessing something and seeing it happen is a principle that God established at the beginning, as far back as the third verse in our Bibles: "Then God said, 'Let there be light;' and there was light."[202] Before a skerrick of light had fallen on the earth, God had called for illumination and then the light that God saw was determined to be good and the light was separated from

---

[202] Gen. 1:3

darkness. As a result God called the light "day" and he called the darkness "night". Before God's creative power was displayed, God had called the thing into being.

Having prayed for healing, then, and mouthed, "Amen" meaning, "Let there be healing," you are anticipating the healing to take place. You have called healing into being. You can't pray one thing, agree to an event occurring, and then turn around and be fearful or worried about the matter. If you've prayed for your healing, act like it has materialised, even when it is not so, because when you said "Amen" you had already said you were looking forward to it happening. Thank God for His answer to your prayer even though it looks bleak and like nothing has happened. By saying "Amen" you have entered into a trust relationship with God. Be joyful and praise God for His goodness and mercy to you and thank Him for what He is doing for you. Have an attitude of gratitude.

I want to examine a section of the Bible to impress on you the grave importance that God places on us to show such joyfulness and thankfulness to Him so that he can bless us. I'm referring to the blessings of Mount Gerizim and the curses of Mount Ebal, mountains situated near Nablus in modern Israel. Israel was about to enter the Promised Land after having left Egypt and wandering in the desert for 40 years. God made a covenant with the tribes at this juncture that if they kept His commandments, then a host of blessings would come to them. Contrariwise, if they didn't keep His commandments, severe curses would befall them.

The section amongst the curses that I want to highlight is, "Because you did not serve the LORD your God with joy and gladness of heart, for the abundance of everything, therefore you shall serve your enemies"[203] and then followed a portrayal of how awful that scenario would be. To us this means that if we stop praising God and being joyful in His presence, we are inviting our enemy, Satan, to come into our lives to destroy us.

We learn from this passage that joyfulness and gratitude is a principle that God demands of us. It is a principle that is taken up throughout the Bible in all sorts of contexts: in worship and in giving, for example, but it is in the context of healing that I want to focus.

When you have said "Amen" to a prayer you have stepped into the arena of faith. In faith you are joyful. In faith you believe God for what you have asked. Worry and anxiety have gone. You have cast all of your cares onto the Sustainer of all life and so you can only be left with joyfulness.

Jesus reminded His disciples not to worry about what they

---

[203] Deut. 28: 47-48

would eat or drink: "Do not seek what you should eat or what you should drink, nor have an anxious mind.

For all these things the nations of the world seek after: and your Father knows that you need these things."[204]

If God has promised to provide our daily needs, how much more will He meet our needs when we are sick? You are His beloved child resting with your head upon His breast under His wings calling him "Abba" or "Daddy". He is waiting for you to ask Him for healing and to rejoice as you patiently trust Him for that healing.

James also reminds us to not doubt that God will answer our prayers: "Let him ask in faith, with no doubting, for he who doubts is like a wave of the sea driven and tossed by the wind. For let not that man suppose that he will receive anything of the Lord."[205]

James later writes that: "The prayer of faith will save the sick, and the Lord will raise him up. And if he has committed sins, he will be forgiven."[206]

Are you seeing that faith is the key for healing? Saying "Amen" and staunchly believing that it will come to

---

204 Luke 12: 29-30
205 James 1:6-7
206 James 5:15

pass will see healing — that is the promise of scripture. Believe it!

Your faith will overcome the world, the "kosmos", anything that can take away from your service to God. "Whatever is born of God overcomes the world. And this is the victory that has overcome the world — our faith."[207] Your faith will overcome every disease or problem the devil can throw against you. We are in a warfare, which is why Timothy was charged by Paul to "Wage the good warfare, having faith and a good conscience."[208] It is only through faith that God can wield His power.

Paul wrote that it was by taking the "Shield of faith with which you will be able to quench all the fiery darts of the wicked one."[209] Faith can block all the "fiery darts" from Satan. Think about it. The devil is trying to destroy us, he wants to discourage us so that we will walk away from God. "Fiery darts" refers to anything that will lead us to have a negative attitude about God. Sickness is just one of the ways in which the devil wants to see us discouraged, to lose our faith and separate ourselves from God. The last thing the devil wants you to know is to how to use your faith in Jesus as a shield from his attacks.

---

207  1 John 5:4
208  1 Tim.1:18-19
209  Eph.6:16

So what you have said "Amen" to is a statement of your faith. Don't waver on what you have petitioned God for. Stand firm on those words and believe for them to come to pass and rejoice for God has promised that: "Let all those rejoice who put their trust in You: let them ever shout for joy, because You defend them; Let them also who love Your name be joyful in You."[210]

This principle of declaring things that are not as though they are is even found throughout the Old Testament. Isaiah 35 relates what Christ's kingdom would be like with healing and wholeness, spiritually and literally. Verses 3 to 6 are worth quoting:

> Strengthen the weak hands, and make firm the feeble knees.
>
> Say to those who are fearful-hearted, 'Be strong and do not fear!
>
> Behold your God will come with vengeance, with the recompense of God; He will come and save you.'
>
> Then the eyes of the blind shall be opened, and the ears of the deaf shall be unstopped. Then the lame shall leap like a deer, and the tongue of the dumb shall sing.

---

[210] Psa.5:11

Can you see the order of physical healing that Isaiah prophesied? Those who were weak limbed were exhorted to not fear because their God, who keeps us from stumbling and falling, would come and make them whole and then they would be healed and leap like a deer. It was declared over the ailing person that their God would heal them if they trusted in Him and for those who did trust, indeed God did heal them. When we are intentional in our decrees over one another, creating a positive faithful atmosphere, then God can appear and healing can be manifest.

Don't just skip over those verses because you've read them a dozen times before. Stop! We have a prophecy here of what it would be like in Jesus' kingdom that would be established when He first came to this earth. This isn't some future event. This is for the here and now. I know that because these very words were quoted for the present time.

The writer of the Hebrews, probably Paul, had Isaiah in mind when he wrote in Hebrews 12:12-13: "Therefore strengthen the hands that hang down, and the feeble knees, and make straight paths for your feet, so that what is lame may not be dislocated (it means shunned, forsaken or avoided), but rather be healed."

The Christian is being told to be single minded and forthright and trust unwaveringly in our God who can save or heal. Walk a straight path — don't be double-minded or indecisive in your belief for your God to come and make the lame person whole. Don't complain. Only when a Christian sees distinctly the race they are on, and looks to the Author and Finisher of the race, our God who comes with vengeance against all the afflictions of the enemy can there be healing for those who are lame and physically infirm.

Just on that point of being intentional and purposeful in our decrees, we have an insightful narrative in the Biblical record in 2 Kings 13:18-19. There is a little detail in this story that could easily be missed.

Joash was a wicked king over Israel who ran to the prophet, Elisha, who was sick on his deathbed, and asked him to do something because Syria was threatening to destroy Israel. Firstly, Elisha told him to shoot an arrow out of the window and told Joash that this symbolised a victory against the Syrians at Aphek. Next Elisha told Joash to take the quiver full of arrows and strike the ground with them. Joash struck the ground three times and stopped. Elisha was angry with Joash for his half-hearted response and said that Israel would only defeat Syria three times, but would not wipe them out.

The lesson for us is that if we are lackadaisical towards God's promises, if we lack zeal and fervour, if we don't really believe and trust in what we are doing, then God's original promises to us won't be fulfilled. God wants people who really trust in Him, people who pursue Him at every turn. God wants to hear us being confident and straightforward in His ability to heal.

Don't listen to the devil and his lies that God won't answer your prayer. God promised healing and you may have to wait for it, but it will happen because God is faithful. Sarah, remember, waited 70 years for Isaac to be born because she saw God as faithful. She rested on the promise of God. She wasn't frazzled that it wasn't happening. She may have waited a long time for it to happen, but not for a moment did she think that it wouldn't happen.

The Bible is full of women with faith like that who have believed the promises of God. Jochebed, who hid Moses in the bulrushes. Miriam, Moses' sister who watched over Moses in the bulrushes. Jael who struck down Sisera with a tent peg. Esther who saved a nation. Mary, the mother of Jesus. All of these believed and accepted the promises of God.

Even in Jesus' human heritage through Mary we have some women who many have wondered why they were there, but they were there because they demonstrated unwavering faith in God to do what he said he would do. One had such faith that she did something extraordinarily risky — but the story is squalid.

When the patriarch Jacob was dying he blessed his 12 sons. He said of Judah that the sceptre, or royal line, would not depart from Judah, nor the ruler's staff from between his feet until he to whom it belongs would come, that is, Jesus. Jacob was divinely predicting that the Messiah would be born through Judah's lineage.

A woman named Tamar was married to Judah's oldest son who was so wicked that God killed him. According to the Law, Tamar was then given to the second son, but again he was killed for his wickedness. Tamar should have been given to the last and youngest son to produce an heir, but Judah was afraid that Tamar was cursed so he didn't give him to her as a husband. Tamar saw this and knew that the royal line was dependent on Judah producing an heir through her as the oldest daughter-in-law so she dressed herself as a prostitute and seduced her father-in-law, Judah, and from that union produced twin sons, one of whom was in the lineage of Jesus.

Tamar knew the divine promise to Judah. She stopped at nothing to see that God's word eventuated. She risked being burnt to death for acting like a harlot, but she was determined to see that promise come true and, despite the sinful way that it all happened, God honoured her faithfulness to Him and His word and included her in the genealogy of Jesus.

Just as Tamar held onto a promise and pursued it single-mindedly, we have a promise of our wholeness from sin and disease in Jesus and we need to pursue God for that promise with a passion that knows no bounds. Our pursuit of God and the love relationship we have with Him is illustrated in the Song of Solomon. This is a fabulous book of poetry about the love relationship, but it is also a very different take on romance and desire. The beloved husband keeps on disappearing and his love-besotted wife keeps on devotedly searching for him until, despite obstacles, he is finally found and their love is consummated. This is exactly like it is with knowing God. One minute you are in intimate communion and the next minute He has gone and there appears to be no answer when you approach Him.

God wants you to tirelessly pursue Him. This is a great theme of scripture. If you query this, just check the number of times and the context in the Bible of the use of words relating to zeal, desire, eagerness, enthusiasm, commitment, dedication, earnestness or faithfulness.

If God has promised something in His word and you want that from God, pursue Him and show Him you are serious. Get passionate. Show intense fervour. Be enthusiastic in your worship of our God and don't worry about what others may think. David did and even though he was despised for it by Michal, his wife, he didn't stop. He wrote that the

"Zeal for Your house has eaten me up."[211] Being half-hearted doesn't work with God!

Your enthusiastic faith and belief in God's promises will be accounted as righteousness, but being zealous for God will have a price to pay.

---

[211] Psa. 69:9

# Chapter 23
# It's a Wild Journey

*"God will save us from the fowler's snare, from the deadly pestilence. We will not fear the terror of night nor the arrow that flies by day, nor the pestilence that stalks in the darkness, nor the plague that destroys at midday. No harm or disaster will come near you because He will command His angels concerning you, to guard you in all your ways. They will lift you up in their hands so that you will not strike your foot against a stone."*
(Psa. 91:3,5,10-12)

If the devil attacks you, you may be sure you are doing something right! My husband, Pete, once said to the persecuted Chinese Christian, Samuel Lamb, that in Australia we have no persecution and instantly Samuel asked him, "What are you doing wrong?"

Pete talks about visiting underground churches overseas where Christians are suffering for their faith. While those Christians spoke about being persecuted for Jesus, they were all on fire for God. People can't be nominal Christians in a country where identifying as a Christian can mean life or death. Having made the decision to be a Christian, these people were prepared to give even their lives for Jesus. We in the West need to catch their fire for Jesus who is worth dying for. We have a comfortable road and therein lies the trap to have a comfortable Jesus.

When you are contending for Jesus there will be opposition from the forces of evil. The devil has tried time and again to take me out. We are in a full-on war and we have a powerful opponent, but we have a much more powerful ally in Jesus whose power you can call upon, no matter what the situation.

For some reason the devil has seen me as a threat from my infancy.

As a pre-schooler an abduction attempt by a band of itinerant gypsies was foiled by my vigilant mother who ran after the truck in which I was being held.

As a child a man unsuccessfully attempted to lure me into his vehicle, but he later enticed and killed a young boy.

As a teenager I was grabbed by two young men at a bus stop and dragged towards their car, but managed to escape.

I was once attempting to cross Pitt Street, Sydney on a busy Friday afternoon. I can't explain it but I physically felt evil all around me, and not knowing what to pray for, I prayed in the spirit. I couldn't cross the one-way street where I was attempting to because of the heavy traffic so I walked up to the lights and crossed there. No sooner had I crossed the road when 20 tonnes of the building façade fell right where I had been standing. Not a person had been killed because the lights were still red for the oncoming traffic.

I was in a light aircraft when the engine stalled going over a mountain and, terrifyingly, took its time to restart.

I rounded a corner as a car exploded in Tehran.

I was sitting on a public bench shortly before a suicide-bomber killed people there in Jerusalem.

I was trekking up a rocky outcrop in Wilpena Pound in South Australia early one morning when a juvenile mallee brown snake slithered out to where I was about to put my foot. On every count I was dead! A juvenile snake's venom is more potent than that of an adult, a cold snake is more likely to attack than a warm snake that can slither away, the mallee brown (or king brown) snake makes it to the top 10 of Australia's venomous snakes and I was about to threaten one by stamping on it! God gave me the grace to rebalance myself on one foot and to hold that pose long enough for the snake to ever so slowly slither away.

I used to be first to arrive at work in the city and would swipe the locked doors for me to enter. Twice strangers have slipped through the closing glass doors to the street and followed me into the lift. Both times I instantly leapt out of the lift and called for help. One man was found standing and waiting in the dark for me on my level.

I was battling dumping waves as I was swimming around a headland when I suddenly had severe debilitating cramps in both legs — a result of being on chemo at the time. I couldn't move them at all. Pete had been a lifesaver and he literally saved my life that day.

I was short-cutting through the red shirt brigade in Bangkok hours before a person was shot dead in that spot.

I was in a Thai school when knife-wielding bandits arrived wanting blood.

I have been pursued across Thai provinces by a murderous Thai man and a van-load of armed thugs after we had informed him that the funding from Australia for his orphanage was ending because we had discovered gross misappropriation of funds.

I was on a road in Thailand when an oncoming truck hit the centre island and the attached trailer disconnected, flew into the air and landed directly in front of our car.

Need I go on? I only tell you this to embolden you that the devil has no power over you until Jesus calls you home. Be bold and face our evil opponent with the power of the Holy Spirit within you.

We haven't been given a spirit of fear but of power, and of love, and of a sound mind. We need to go out and claim the land that has been given to us. May we go forward with a fire and passion to preach the gospel to all who are perishing and demonstrate the power of who Jesus is and what He has done for us. The victory He gave us cannot be kept close to us because Jesus promised that His Spirit would be given to us so that we would have power to witness.[212]

While we experience God when we are alone with Him, intimacy with God also comes when we cling to Him in difficult times of witnessing and battling our malevolent opponent. I have actually seen amazing answers to prayer when I have cleaved to Him in those trying times — there is a real closeness to God when you witness. Walking with God will be the adventure of your life as you battle with all the arsenal that heaven has given us against an evil, deceptive and unscrupulous opponent.

God loves us. If we dwell in His shelter we are promised that He will be our sanctuary. God didn't promise removal

---

[212] Acts 1:8

from trouble, but He did promise refuge under His shadow. We have such a lovely Jesus who always proves Himself to be a mighty Deliverer, only planning the best things for us.

Those words were brought vividly home to me recently. I had been sharing the power in the name of Jesus over all the threats of the enemy and as I was walking back home along a level concrete path with flat, "sensible" shoes on, I was supernaturally lifted up and thrown flat on my face so quickly that my nose hit the ground. I didn't even have time to put my arms out. True to God's word, God's angels protected me and I didn't break anything or have even a scrape or bruise. A woman passing by saw it all happen and exclaimed in disbelief, "What on earth just happened?"

That incident roused me to finish my story, to give you the knowledge of who you are in Christ and the power you have over all the weapons of the enemy and to enjoy all the blessings that have been given to us in Jesus. I want you to just believe God and whatever healing or petition you are asking God for, will happen. The greatest things will start to happen if you will only believe God, without doubting. Our God is real in His saving and healing power today. He is the same Jesus yesterday, today and forever. He saves and heals today just like He did 2,000 years ago and He wants to be your Saviour and Healer.

You have unlimited "dunamis" power available to you. It

is not your power. It is the power of the King of the entire universe — "Yours is the kingdom and the power and the glory forever."[213] God's power and authority is there for you to have "Power and authority over all demons, and to cure diseases."[214] God's divine power has been given to us for all things that relate to this life and godliness.[215] God wants to show His power through you, but there is one condition: You must acknowledge Him as your Lord and Saviour; you must set your love upon Him and then He will honour you.[216]

To do that you must realise that you are weak and that you can do nothing without Him. Like Jacob wrestling with the angel and asking for a blessing,[217] our wrestling with the man of God will extract everything that hinders His control of us and will reduce us to complete surrender. Then, and only then, can we stand when we inevitably wrestle with the "Principalities, powers, the rulers of darkness of this age and spiritual hosts of wickedness in the heavenly places."[218] It is only when you have surrendered that God's strength will be revealed for Jesus Himself declared: "My power is perfected in weakness."[219]

---

213  Matt. 6:13
214  Luke 9:1
215  2 Pet. 1:3
216  Psa. 91:14-15
217  Gen. 32:24
218  Eph. 6:12
219  2 Cor. 12:9

"I bow my knees to the Father of our Lord Jesus Christ, from whom the whole family in heaven and earth is named, that He would grant you, according to the riches of His glory, to be strengthened with might through His Holy Spirit in the inner man, that Christ may dwell in your hearts through faith; that you, being rooted and grounded in love, may be able to comprehend with all the saints what is the width and length and depth and height — to know the love of Christ, which passes knowledge that you may be filled with all the fullness of God.

Now to Him who is able to do exceedingly abundantly above all that we ask or think, according to the power that works in us, to Him be the glory in the church by Christ Jesus to all generations, forever and ever. Amen."[220]

---

[220] Eph. 3:14-21

www.ingramcontent.com/pod-product-compliance
Lightning Source LLC
Chambersburg PA
CBHW030253010526
44107CB00053B/1699